Start & Run a
Rural Computer Consulting Business

John D. Deans

Self-Counsel Press
(a division of)
International Self-Counsel Press Ltd.
USA   Canada

Self-Counsel Press acknowledges the financial support of the Government of Canada through the Book Publishing Industry Development Program (BPIDP) for our publishing activities.

Printed in Canada.

First edition: 2006

Library and Archives Canada Cataloguing in Publication

Deans, John D. (John David), 1963–
Start & run a rural computer consulting business / John D. Deans.

    (Self-counsel business series)
    ISBN-13: 978-1-55180-725-6
    ISBN-10: 1-55180-725-4

    1. Electronic data processing consultants. 2. New business enterprises. I. Title. II. Title: Start and run a rural computer consulting business. III. Series.

HD69.C6D42 2006   004.068'1   C2006-903146-0

Self-Counsel Press
(a division of)
International Self-Counsel Press Ltd.

1704 North State Street	1481 Charlotte Road
Bellingham, WA 98225	North Vancouver, BC V7J 1H1
USA	Canada

To my wife, Beth, who supported my wild idea to escape the big city and settle down in an environment completely foreign to us both. The early years were a challenge as we had to adapt to the differences in both our personal and professional lives. She's my trouper!

Contents

Notice to Readers

Prologue

It was early one afternoon in the summer of 1998, and I was already stuck in first gear sitting in Houston traffic. The analysts at the primary client site I was supporting had just called my cell phone for the sixth time concerning router stability. Having worked in information technology since 1981, I was at the top of my game and leading one of the largest and earliest Gigabit Ethernet installations in the world for our client, Compaq Computer Corporation. The high stress was causing my chest to tighten, which made me remember a few of my peers who had bypasses (or even died from heart attacks) in their late thirties and early forties while supporting enterprise-level computer networks. I felt I was going down the same path — sitting there looking at red brake lights brought to mind the movie *Falling Down*, starring Michael Douglas. The breaking point was fast approaching.

To avoid the impending road rage, I let my mind drift back to a few weeks before when I'd spent a Saturday with one of our sales guys, Tom S., who owned an 80-acre ranch a few miles west of Katy, Texas. I remembered the quiet, the space, the freedom, and the absence of the frantic pace that pushed me every weekday. We went shooting, fishing, and then drank a few beers on the porch while the sun set, and the only sound around was the birds and the crickets.

My tranquil daydream was blown away by the deep, booming stereo of the car next to me and then my cell phone ringing from a client calling from the far side of town — surely with a problem that needed to be fixed immediately.

The tightness in my chest was turning to chest pains, and I was rapidly reaching my boiling point. I was just plain tired of the rat race of city life and big-company computer support. I was sick of the stupid office e-mail wars and the meetings that lasted for hours where everyone finally left with so-called action items. The traffic in Houston, like in many large metropolitan areas in America, was getting worse every year. I was tired of having to be armed with my .45 handgun every time I went to get gas or groceries. With the property taxes going up 10 percent every year (which amounts to taxes doubling after seven years), the tax escrow for our home in a small city on the southwest side of Houston was more than the principal and interest payment on a mortgage. I was also sick of dealing with clients that were lawyers or liberals since I didn't trust either group.

That's when it hit me: I've got to get out of this place before it kills me or I do something very dangerous.

I had lived in Houston all my life and knew the city and fast-paced lifestyle well. The network integration company I'd helped to found, Paranet, had just been sold to Sprint, and my little chunk of the cash buyout was working well for me and my wife. The next thing we knew, we had bought a 115-acre ranch near Brenham and started spending the weekends there so I could chill out and slow my ever-growing burnout from the computer consulting industry. On Friday nights on the way out of town, I could actually feel my body relax. When we crossed the Brazos River into Washington County, the week's stress would fade away.

Those 48 hours would pass way too quickly, though, because the Sunday night drives back to Houston made things even worse. My sweet wife, Beth, and my 12-year-old son from my first marriage could both sense me tightening up as we neared the big-city lights.

The weekends were not enough. I wanted to be full time in the country on our ranch — away from that urban meat grinder that made me a good living but was sucking the life out of me. The negotiations began with me trying to convince my city-girl wife to move out of the fourth largest city in the United States (and away from her close family) to a small, conservative rural community. We were expecting our first child when she agreed to leave Houston and move to Brenham — I could now see a light at the end of the tunnel.

At the end of 1998, we sold our small, tear-down Bellaire home for the dirt under it. The whole area was going through one of those booms with yuppies buying older, small homes and replacing them with big, half-million-dollar brick boxes. We took our profits, and after a grand send-off, headed to Brenham, leaving behind my consulting firm, Paranet, and some of the best memories of my professional life.

I didn't realize it at the time, but I had taken the first step toward becoming a rural computer consultant.

PART 1

BACKGROUND OF A RURAL COMPUTER CONSULTANT

1

Escaping the Urban IT-Support Rat Race

This book is a step-by-step guide for computer support professionals working high-stress information technology jobs in large cities. It's intended for the ones who plan to or just dream about moving out of the city to a small town — and actually making a living as an independent rural computer consultant.

This was exactly what I did in 1999, when I left one of Houston's most successful network integration firms, moved to rural Brenham, Texas, and started a one-man computer consulting firm.

Most IT jobs are located in cities. Compensation is good — but there's a price to be paid for it. There's also an alternative, which I'll tell you about later in this chapter.

Urban IT Grinder: The Dark Side of a Bright Industry

We've all seen the IT guys with their identification badges hanging from their necks on a vendor-provided band and a cluster of smartphone, PDA, and beeper on their belts. Their faces have a concentrated look, and they all walk fast to get to their next technology firefight.

These are the hardware and software professionals who keep corporate America's bits moving in an orderly and dependable fashion. Many have degrees, most have certifications, and some have both. The vast majority, around 90 percent, are men, and most of them are younger than 40 years of age. Their employers are usually companies with 50 or more employees and are generally located in cities with populations of at least 50,000. The denser the city's population, the more information infrastructure is required to serve the workers, which in turn increases the need for information technology talent.

This is why the mother lode of IT positions is in metropolitan areas. I started my IT career at Houston's Control Data Corporation in 1981 and was fortunate not to be transferred or to have to chase a job to another big city, which allowed me to maintain strong contacts with my family and longtime friends. Only by choice in the late 1990s did I move out of the big city — which led me to write this book.

So if you are or want to be an IT person, odds are you are or will be working in a metro-area company dealing with a boss and some level of traffic. Along with city living comes the higher cost of housing, taxes, and other services, as well as a higher rate of crime. Though many urban IT pros may work downtown, they probably live in the suburbs where housing is more affordable. This is where the traffic comes into play, since many IT pros have an average 30-minute commute each way to work.

The younger tech-support staffers just getting started usually get apartments close to work so they can respond fast to work needs, like being "on call." As they age, get married, and have kids, their home square-footage requirement grows, which pushes them farther out of the core areas into more affordable housing markets — which in turn increases their commute time.

These are the issues for the internal support professionals who have a single fixed place of employment with little travel required on the job. The other group of cyber-hounds, however, includes hourly billable consultants and contractors, who have to go where the short-term technical work is located. Many times they will actually fly out Sunday night or early Monday morning to a remote client site, work like dogs all week, and then fly back late Friday afternoon to their homes. During the workweek, they fight the city's unfamiliar traffic patterns and deal with the hidden crime dangers while driving a rented car and finally crashing in a lonely hotel room, which may or may not have a working high-speed Internet connection.

Traffic hurts IT people more than workers in most other industries because there are so many instances when we have to make a second trip to the work site to fix a problem or to work on a project outside of prime time. During some troubleshooting events, I've had to make multiple trips back and forth to work, chasing an intermittent networking problem that seemed to pop up again only after I arrived back home. It should come as no surprise that big IT job centers such as San Francisco, Los Angeles, Seattle, San Jose, Houston, Dallas, Atlanta, New York, Chicago, and Boston comprise the top ten worst traffic areas in the United States.

I make such a big deal out of the traffic issue because it really is a big deal. Sitting in traffic while commuting to and from work is wasted time. It is frustrating, upsetting, and sometimes maddening. I have not only witnessed but also (unfortunately) participated in road rage on more than one occasion.

Basically, commuting to our IT jobs really inhales immensely (i.e., it sucks!), and traffic congestion in the urban and metropolitan areas in which we work is constantly getting worse. Keep reading, and I can show you an alternative to your daily gridlock and gruel.

Once you actually get to work, it is likely you have a single primary superior or boss to deal with on a daily basis. You hope this person is a moral, fair, and understanding human being who is familiar with your job requirements, your professional capabilities, and your personal commitments and needs. I have been very fortunate at the companies I've worked for to have had great bosses who not only treated me fairly, but also mentored me and looked out for my best interest. They all wanted me to progress, learn, and eventually move on to bigger and better things. I was constantly given opportunities to grow my skill sets, and my mentors nurtured my personal communication techniques to better deal with customers and peers.

I was lucky, but many others are not so fortunate and have to deal with bosses, superiors, team leaders, and other higher-ups who seem to be complete jerks. This brings me to another point of concern common to many urban IT-support positions: the "single point of economic failure." The vast majority of IT professionals — not to mention most employees of companies in any industry — have a single boss to report to who has almost unilateral control over their immediate future. That one boss can limit your professional growth and opportunities, or worse, can terminate your employment and cut off 100 percent of your income without warning.

Let me emphasize this point. It only takes one obnoxious manager assigned as your superior to stop your paychecks and send you home, stunned and suddenly unemployed. How much of the money you've saved for the kids' college or a new home will now be needed just to pay the mortgage, car notes, and other bills? Will you have to move and take the kids out of their school midyear? Can you even sell the house now and recoup what you've put into it? Is the IT market in your area already saturated with pros like yourself barely holding onto their jobs? How long can you go until the next paycheck is deposited into your soon-to-be-shrinking bank account?

This may sound like doom and gloom talk, but I have heard and seen it from too many of my IT peers since the technology industry crash of 2000. Since many of us are monstrous consumers, we have the bills and debt to go with that high earning and spending lifestyle. We all seem to need the largest house we can afford at the time of purchase, multiple SUVs, and expensive vacations just to get away from the computer world at least once a year. All this costs more than we can usually pay in cash, so we put it on credit. But lose your job and this single point of economic failure will kill you financially and possibly devastate your fiscal plans for years.

Becoming a rural computer consultant can not only get you away from the metropolitan traffic nightmare, but can also eliminate this single point of economic failure. There are thousands of small rural communities similar to the one I am flourishing in. Note that 80 percent of workers are employed by small companies with less than 50 employees. You can be the IT pro for a number of those small companies in a rural town or cluster of towns far away from the big city.

Later in this book I will describe in detail how to get these small businesses as paying clients, effectively getting multiple monthly paychecks instead of having to rely on one source for 100 percent of your income. Remember, this is real work for real people and not some B.S. work-at-home scheme or MLM (multi-level-marketing) plan. You already have an existing IT skill set. I will explain how you can expand that skill set to serve small businesses in rural areas — allowing you to change your life.

Rural Computer Consulting: A Brand-New Niche

A rural computer consultant is the jack-of-all-computer-trades. He or she has to be able to fix, configure, install, test, and troubleshoot everything and anything electronic that businesses use on a day-to-day basis, and do all this for numerous customers that make up a client base.

During my years as an urban enterprise-level consultant, I never imagined doing what I do now or doing it where I do it. My perception during the 1990s was that only big cities had enough computer-related jobs and projects to support full-time information technology personnel. What I've learned is that a small town (or cluster of small towns within a 30-mile radius) big enough to warrant a Wal-Mart and a McDonald's is fertile ground for computer consulting experts.

I grant you that most small-town environments will only support one or two multi-skilled consultants, but odds are that should you decide to become a rural computer consultant, you won't find much competition. One of the reasons I can say this with confidence is that while I was researching this book, I was not able to find any other books describing IT or computer consulting in rural areas. There were, however, numerous books in both hardcover and paperback related to general consulting, IT consulting, and starting small businesses in various IT fields. The common thread to all these books was the need for medium-to-large metropolitan areas as a marketplace.

Another way I learned that there are not many computer consultants working solely in rural environments was by roaming chat rooms and newsgroups. What I've discovered is that ever since the IT bust of 2000, many of my peers have had to really scrounge for work just to pay their bills. They've had to take almost anything, anywhere, even if it required flying out to the client site on Sunday nights and back again late Friday afternoons. Others have simply given up and taken work in non-IT environments. The past five years have certainly culled many single-skill-set workers and/or poor performers from the IT industry.

Rarely, if ever, did I hear or read of urban IT professionals leaving the city for the country and successfully providing computer consulting and services. If you're willing to accept some risk, however, the rewards can be great.

I was lucky enough to be able to take all of 1999 off from the IT industry so I could investigate various agribusinesses that could be supported on my 115-acre ranch in Brenham. After learning about multiple types of farming and ranching business models such as raising chickens, goats, and horses, or growing fruit trees or cut flowers, I realized that farming and ranching were not my cup of tea.

During those nine months of testing both plant crops and animal raising, I ran the numbers on Excel and discovered a disheartening fact about agribusinesses. Most of these farming and ranching enterprises require large capital investment, are high risk due to uncontrollable factors such as weather, require hard outdoor work seven days a week, and have a very low payout at the end of the year. This is with no major disasters such as drought or illness.

So in 2000, despite having turned down multiple requests for me to do some consulting work in Houston and Austin, I did finally accept a couple of short-term contracts.

Even at that time, I didn't believe that Brenham or even all of Washington County would have enough consulting projects to keep me busy, but I decided to start looking for opportunities locally in our new small hometown. Chapter 13 will address in detail how I was able to get my original 12 clients.

As time went on, I was able to gather more rural clients, and by late 2002, I was able to stop taking new Houston and Austin clients entirely. By early 2003, my 40-plus active rural clients were keeping me hopping, so I handed off my remaining Houston and Austin clients to my consultant friends. My billable time was consistently hitting over $10K per month from Washington County clients alone. I had arrived at a small-company plateau I never thought possible just a couple of years before.

It was then, around 2003, when I fully grasped what I had become — a rural computer consultant. I had not planned, projected, researched, or read about this new niche. I had just developed it in real time based on the computing needs of the local businesses.

The exciting thing about being the jack-of-all-IT-trades in the country is that you are doing many different things all day long, and you are rarely at one client's site for the majority of the day. My normal schedule consists of four, and sometimes up to eight or even ten client-site visits in one day. This would be nearly impossible in a large metro area due to travel times between clients and traffic limitations. Back in the 1990s in Houston, it was rare indeed when I could visit three clients in a day, let alone four or more.

Another good thing about small-town clients is that they are mostly on an eight- to nine-hour day, five days a week. Some of the larger ones may have a second evening shift that you might have to support, but that is rare. This is a major benefit for a rural computer consultant — being able to work from 8 a.m. to 5 p.m., Monday through Friday, and still be close to the house or your kids' school.

Some days will start out with you having to resolve e-mail problems for Client A, then driving ten or so miles to the neighboring town to troubleshoot backup problems for Client B. Remember that those ten miles will take only about ten minutes, driving through country roads with nice hay fields and cows to look at instead of glaring red taillights and tall buildings. If you do your planning right, Client C is in that same neighboring town and needs you to pick up an old Windows 2000 PC and upgrade it to Windows XP Pro overnight and return it the next morning.

Some days will be project days with specific tasks and jobs to perform on a schedule. Those days are nice, since you are able to focus, plan, and have the required hardware and software on hand. Other days will be in what I call "interrupt mode" or "firefighting mode," when you go from problem to problem, fixing the computer and network glitches that seem to crop up in threes. Usually, though, after you get a decent client load, you will have days that go as planned and others that are dynamic. You'll learn to prioritize the level of need, rating it somewhere between an emergency work-stoppage situation and a nice-to-have improvement. Deciding which client to hit next when your schedule gets full is almost an art in itself since you are trying to keep the travel time down and the on-site billing time up.

As I will describe later in this book, the best way to hold on to new clients is by being available and successfully fixing a computer-related problem the business is currently having. If you get a call from a small-business owner who is having network problems and is a friend of one of your current clients, you have got to jump on that one immediately!

Just like any other small-business owner, you must wear many corporate hats. Besides being a computer consultant, you need to also be your own bookkeeper, salesperson, marketing representative, and bill collector, all wrapped into one. When the phone isn't ringing and your project list is short, your new job for that day or week is marketing!

At the end of the month, with hopefully dozens of invoices to send out, you recheck your billable time and all hardware/software sales, add any applicable taxes, and get those bills in the mail to your clients. Don't forget about your company's bills, since they collect up in your in-box just as fast as your personal bills.

Rural computer consulting wasn't the career I started out in. Nonetheless, my former career in big-city IT was excellent preparation for what I'm doing now. And that's the topic of the next chapter.

2

The Making of a Rural Computer Consultant

I got into the IT industry very early in my working life. I had been a pretty good student in high school, but after graduating, I quickly discovered that college was not for me. However, I had to let my parents know that, so with my stomach in knots, I met with them and told them that I was dropping out of college. I had never really wanted to go in the first place.

My dad, surprisingly, said, "OK. Now it's time for you to go find a job." Since I was 18 and still at home, he also informed me that I would immediately start paying him rent and it was due at the end of the month, so I'd better get after it.

That was what I wanted to hear. I may have disliked school, but I loved to work and get paid for it. I was ready for the future.

Early Career and Successes

Now that I was out of high school and not going to college, I knew I had to find an industry that offered strong opportunities to someone with few skills. Jean Long, a long-time family friend, worked at Key People Personnel, which happened to be in the same building as Control Data Corporation (CDC). She told my dad to tell me to drop by her office, and she would get me an interview at CDC. Since all I had was a high school diploma and a strong work ethic, I was willing to take anything.

After three interviews in a row that same morning, I landed a job as a process control clerk working for CDC in the Galleria area of Houston. This was great since it was only three miles from my parents' home (where I was still living) and I was making a whopping $800 a month.

This was my first information technology (IT) job and it consisted of mainly taking the printouts and plots off large printers and plotters, feeding computer cards into high-speed readers, and mounting nine-track reel tape on rows of six-foot-high tape drives.

Since the rent my dad was charging me was low and I didn't really have any other bills or debt, I spent most of my money over the next year taking flying lessons at Houston's hobby airport on the weekends. And on weekdays, after work ended at 4 p.m., I'd run home for dinner and then back up to work to take great computer courses offered by my employer on the Plato Learning Network.

They had a whole curriculum for computer hardware and software that was free to all employees. I ate these courses up, taking as many as I could … topics covering programming languages, hardware trouble-shooting, and software design. After six months and with more than 20 completed courses behind me, a light went on in my head: I really dig this computer thing!

Just after my one-year anniversary with CDC, my boss offered me a promotion to billing processing operator. This was an awesome opportunity offered to me, given than two of my other workmates had been in the process control room longer than I had. Dad told me it was because of all the late-night course work I had done, which was all logged and reported to management on a monthly basis. Odds are he was right about that, just like he was all the other times.

Those late-night courses continued to pay off for me because over the next year, I used what I had learned to streamline CDC's bill-processing system. I was so successful in this that I managed to get the whole process down from ten hours a day to only two.

For some reason, I kept this accomplishment quiet for a few months. This allowed me the time to create extra reports with color graphs showing the billing activity, which the managers loved. It also allowed me to sneak out of work early (quite often) to surf in Galveston during storm season, which was the only time the waves were rideable.

The weekday surfing is what got me caught. Noticing the tan skin and sun-bleached blond hair, my boss checked up on my processing logs and found that I had optimized my job-processing time down to less than part-time hours. He called me in to meet with him and two other managers in his office, and I thought I was fired. I confessed my prime-time surfing escapades, highlighting all the extra graphs and timely billing reports, and hoped not to get slammed too hard.

Instead, they told me to move my stuff to the customer service department. They were promoting me to Systems Analyst, along with giving me a substantial raise!

Holy cow! I made Systems Analyst in two years, right out of high school!

During that last year at CDC, I spent most of my time working user problems over the phone at a desk in customer service. It was a good learning experience, but it got old real fast, yapping on the phone all day and not having my hands on the hardware and hacking out software.

This was back in 1984, and the oil industry was hurting in Houston. Since I was still watching the billing processes, I happened to notice a significant downturn in mainframe time-sharing services, which were CDC's bread and butter.

My girlfriend's best friend got me in for an interview at J. S. Nolan and Associates in West Houston. After a few weeks of pursuing it, I got the job, and left CDC just before they started laying off people.

J. S. Nolan was a group of a dozen or so PhDs who had developed an oil reservoir simulation program and made millions marketing it all over the world. My new job was to manage Nolan's in-house VAX/VMS computers, and port the massive 150,000-line Fortran program onto every scientific mainframe and minicomputer made. This was the ultimate learning opportunity, since the first thing Nolan did was send me to Intel and later to Convex to learn the Unix operating system.

The three years I spent with Nolan gave me tons of experience in programming, computer management, hardware troubleshooting, and software debugging techniques. Porting the program was basically taking a nine-track tape of source code, loading it up on the mainframe, creating the JCL to run the jobs, compiling the code, linking all the binary libraries, and utilizing the proprietary capabilities of the mainframe. These capabilities included double precision, vectorization, and parallelization on supercomputers such as Cray, IBM, CDC, Convex, Intel Hypercube, and many others. I was also exposed to the first version of Ethernet 802.3 10Base5 over thick wire coax cabling, which was my first real local area networking experience.

The last year got rough after J. S. Nolan sold out to Dresser and the bean counters took over. As with CDC, I could see the writing on the wall, and started looking for a new position.

In 1987, an opportunity came along with CogniSeis Development, who offered me a job as manager of computer operations. This consisted of managing seven people and more than thirty medium-to-large computers and mainframes. The good thing is that I was in management and making more than

$40K a year; the bad thing was that during that next year, I went through both a divorce and the death of my father.

The six prior years had been nothing but bits and bytes, with all issues black and white. There was no gray in my world back then. Management was entirely new to me, and I was just a babe in the woods. Right off the bat, I had two hardware guys and four computer operators reporting to me, while we all supported approximately 200 users working on VT100 terminals connected to Digital Equipment Corporation (DEC) VAX/VMS mainframe computers, along with 50-plus smaller Unix-based computers and workstations.

Over my fours years at CogniSeis, my divorce was finalized, I buried my dad, dated and broke up with multiple girlfriends, and actually started being a dad to my young son, who was with me for the standard visitation periods doled out by Texas law. After paying off the five-figure debt from the divorce and finally moving out of my sister's place, I was able to buy a small but nice home in Bellaire, which is a small city within Houston.

In 1991, my nephew had freshly returned from his Air Force service in Saudi Arabia during Desert Shield and Storm. We celebrated by going to Hawaii and surfing for seven days and drinking for seven nights. When I got back, I had a call on my answering machine to contact a Michael Holthouse, who wanted to interview me for a position with a new company he was starting, called Paranet.

The meeting with Holthouse's right-hand man, Steve Ough, went great as far as technical interviews go, and then it was onto

Holthouse himself and things got interesting. He explained to me that the goal of Paranet (with just seven employees at the time) was to hire IT experts, get support contacts, and grow as fast as possible. With a five- to seven-year time frame, his plan was to either sell Paranet or go public with it and take a big payoff for himself and the start-up team, of which I would be a critical member — if I joined up now. He scribbled out a $55K salary with a possible if not probable end payout of over $2,000,000 if we hit our objectives.

This rocked my world! By this time, I had it made at CogniSeis, with a great crew that kept all the systems running well. I had it easy and smooth with a decent salary of $47K, working less than 40 hours a week at a location less than four miles from my home. Choosing a start-up company over the safe, secure, and happy environment that had nurtured me over the past four years was a hard decision.

But there was one thing in Paranet's favor: my fear that in five years, I would regret not having recognized this chance as the opportunity it was. After a weekend of deep thought, talks with friends, and several glasses of wine, I accepted Paranet's offer the next Monday.

The Paranet Days

I'm detailing my time at Paranet because it was a turning point in my life, one that allowed me to later make another major life-changing decision — landing me in my current career as a rural computer consultant.

The first year at Paranet was frantic, exciting, exhausting, and even debilitating. Going from a single-role internal IT support person to an external billable consultant was a major change, and it took all my effort, knowledge, and creative articulation (otherwise know as B.S.). I had spent the past ten years as overhead, never as the core of the business. Starting in May of 1991 at Paranet, I was a designated moneymaker and the primary focus of the company.

Mike Holthouse, the main boss and owner, took charge of management and sales, and Mona Cabler, the office manager, handled everything else. That left the other five of us to be shipped out to IT clients in Houston at a billable rate of $75 to $125 an hour. The first year there was not only hectic, but also highly stressful. Though I successfully completed lucrative contracts at Tenneco, British Petroleum (BP), and GeoQuest, servicing so many new clients felt as intense as acquiring and starting a new job every few weeks.

Holthouse would promise the prospective client that his IT crew could code, fix, integrate, or configure almost any hardware or software problem or project. We were often put in high-expectation situations and sometimes had to read up the night before on a software language, operating system, or computer system we had never even touched, then be able to perform flawlessly the very next day at the client site. This was major pressure and far from the internal IT support environments I was used to.

There were days in those initial months when I thought I wasn't going to be able to handle it, and should maybe bail out and go back to my old, comfortable position at CogniSeis — that would have meant taking a big step back and committing a major error. So to keep myself from running away from the Paranet challenge, I trapped myself by purchasing an expensive used sports car, the payments for which locked me into the new, substantially higher salary. I bought a Porsche 911 Targa that looked great and was a ground rocket. I was also the first one at Paranet to get a cell phone to keep in contact with my new clients. Back in 1991, cell phones were the size of bricks and airtime minutes were outrageously expensive. Between the hot car and the cool phone, I had purposely made myself dependent on Paranet's healthy salary, along with its 10 percent raises, and guaranteed my dedication to this start-up company.

The positive side of their high expectations was that it pushed me to learn fast, adapt quickly, maintain my cool, and interact professionally with new clients and various personalities while consistently accomplishing the assigned IT mission — all skills that would later prove indispensable to me as a rural computer consultant.

By the end of the first year, our initial Paranet team of eight had grown to twenty, and we had billed more than a million dollars. Also, after surviving that first year, I was getting used to going on sales calls, making big technical promises to prospective clients, and then actually accomplishing the project in a timely manner. In other words, my Paranet peers and I were successfully achieving our goals and satisfying our clients, which in turn brought us more business.

The early 1990s at Paranet consisted of fast and furious work along with hard-playing fun. Both the single guys like me and the married fellows worked our butts off during the day and drank together at night back at the office between interviews of potential new Paranet employees. This hard-living fun was especially the case at company parties. I was particularly into it since I was basically single — only getting to see my son on Wednesday nights and every other weekend.

By the end of 1993, the company had grown to around 100 IT professionals billing at a 90 percent utilization rate. That means we were at client sites making money the vast majority of the time. Later that year, I was running two major IT-support teams at both Amoco and British Petroleum that were right across the street from each other. My sales guy had negotiated a dual contract for me to manage a network support team at BP and a desktop support group at Amoco, with an office just for me at each location.

I was constantly running between buildings, attending meetings, and trying to put out technical fires on a billable 10-hours-per-day basis. Needless to say, this was quite demanding and took its toll. Things got even rougher after I handed the smooth-running dual team over to another Paranet colleague and was sent to the infamous Enron to rescue our contract there. It had accumulated $500,000 in unpaid invoices and placed our support presence in jeopardy.

The first month there was pure hell. Enron's corporate culture for contractors and consultants was all stick and no carrot. We were constantly threatened with being fired and were greeted at the beginning of each day with a scowl, a problem list, and a hearty "do this now or else." I worked 12 to 16 hours a day, was on call 24/7, and was harassed by the extremely difficult Enron senior staff, which included Jeffrey Skilling. (A couple of years after the whole company came crashing down in 2001, I took glee in seeing Skilling do the perp walk into federal custody on TV.)

For most of 1994, I was the primary network consultant for Enron's gas and electricity trading floors. Not only did I solve the initial disaster of a situation for Paranet at Enron, but I was also able to resolve multiple network problems and collect the $500,000 they owed us. By the end of my Enron tour of duty, I was developing chest pains, but I was able to pull off a Paranet first by billing over $250,000 in a single year. After a year of dealing with Enron, Paranet actually fired them as a client due to the negative way they treated me. Our founder bragged about that one at a large biweekly company meeting, which made me feel appreciated.

By 1995, Paranet had 22 offices and 500 billable IT professionals making the company $31 million in revenues, and I was getting married! I had met my lovely bride, Beth, at Young Brothers Tae Kwon-Do Martial Arts School in 1993 when she was a second-degree black belt and I was a lowly beginning white belt. After dating a year and a half, we were married and all my buddies from Paranet were at the wedding.

Later in 1995, my first wife and her current husband decided to leave for Dallas with my son, which I fought legally and lost after dropping more than $20,000 in legal fees in less than a month. This hurt badly, and now I had to fly my boy home every other weekend to see him. This grief made me work even harder to help Paranet achieve that big payout goal Holthouse had told me about back in 1991.

Things got mellower after the Enron days. I landed long-term contracts with Amoco, building out their network in a remodeled building in Bay City, and then a two-year-long gig with the Houston computer maker Compaq. By 1997, Paranet was pulling in close to $100 million in revenues with nearly 2,000 employees, and things were popping.

Then the big one hit. Sprint offered us $425 million in cash for a complete purchase of Paranet. We took it, of course, and all ran home to our six-year-old spreadsheets that calculated the worth of our private stock share and options. Though we worker bees only had a small cut of the pie, even little cuts of such a large pie were worth a great deal. Just before the close of the buyout, Sprint pulled a fast one that delayed our payout for three months and discounted the purchase by $50 million, so we settled for $375 million.

Since it was in cash and not stock, the funds were immediately wired to our accounts — and then we learned the meaning of capital gains tax. Some of us paid six and even seven figures in taxes to the federal government, which was very painful.

Though most of the 1990s had been very stressful, 1997 brought me an opportunity to take a new look at things and see what needed to be changed. After almost two decades of working and driving in Houston, the traffic was becoming unbearable. The major vehicle arteries such as Loop 610, I-10, and even the county Beltway 8 were becoming parking lots for most of the day. Carjackings, robberies, and home invasions were constantly on the Houston local news. I had started legally carrying a .45 calibre handgun back in 1995, and almost had to use it on a couple of occasions. Country life was starting to look good.

During the period of the pending Sprint buyout, Beth and I looked at places in the country to the far west and northwest of Houston. Just eight miles west of Brenham, we found a wonderful 115-acre ranch on a hill, with an updated farmhouse built in 1881, a guesthouse, and two barns. After the Sprint deal finally closed in the fall of 1997, we immediately purchased it at a great price from an elderly couple and started spending our weekends up there.

I was still working for Paranet, but was now at Compaq, building one of the first Gigabit Ethernet campus networks, which was also one of the largest at the time. After the buyout, the original start-up group of us had lost interest in growing the company (now called Sprint Paranet) because we were so burnt out and wanted to enjoy life a little.

Our weekends at our new ranch were great for me, but a bit trying for Beth, since she was raised a city girl and liked being close to the malls and her family. I immediately adapted to and adopted the rural life and could not get enough of it. The Friday nights driving to Brenham were full of the anticipation of getting away from my growing dislike of Houston, but the drive back on Sunday evening was full of the dread of returning to traffic, crime, and full-time work for Sprint Paranet.

In April of 1998, another turning point happened when my son's mom moved to Anchorage, Alaska — leaving me with only seeing Dustin three times a year. This loss of time with my 12-year-old son made me have second thoughts about not having any more kids, as I had always told Beth. Soon she was pregnant, and in October of 1998, our beautiful first daughter was born.

That was part of the "deal" I made with my wife to let me sell our Bellaire home, quit Sprint Paranet, and move our new family to our country place, which we had named Seven Eagles Ranch. I gave Beth a new BMW and a grand piano, and she gave us the thumbs up to head to the hills of Brenham, with our gorgeous little baby girl.

My last day at Paranet was December 18, 1998, which just happened to be the same day as our company Christmas party. With Beth at home with her first baby (she wasn't ready to leave her with anyone else yet), I took my son to my last Paranet party, and we had a ball. The goodbyes were heavy and they got me up on the stage in front of hundreds of my Paranet peers and presented me with a nice plaque and a great send-off. Wow — what an excellent ride! In so many ways, Paranet was the greatest company I had ever worked for.

The very next day, we started packing up and moving out to Seven Eagles Ranch to start our new life adventure.

3

Rural Computer Consulting: Is It for You?

The journey that led me to being Washington County's rural computer consultant was not a planned one. If someone had told me back in 1995 that in ten years I would not be designing and building large enterprise-level computer networks supporting thousands of users, but rather be performing a wide range of computer support services for businesses in small towns, I would have called them crazy. Furthermore, if they had then informed me that I would be grossing more than $164,000 a year for these services working out in rural central Texas, I would have called them insane.

When I left Paranet in late 1998, I had enough from the Sprint buyout to last a while, but I honestly had no idea what I was going to do up in Brenham. All I knew was that I had to get out of the city and away from the computer industry that had treated me well but had also burned me out. I basically fell into doing what I do today. I was fortunate enough to see the growing need for computer support in our small town and to turn it to my advantage.

Falling into the Niche

As I've already described, after buying my ranch in 1997 and permanently moving there in late 1998, I discovered I had to give up the idea of making a living from farming and ranching. By the fall of 1999 and on the eve of Y2K, I was getting depressed about my professional future — having found nothing that interested me or that was modestly profitable. I was even starting to miss the computer support world since I had not troubleshot a network or fixed a nonfamily computer in almost a year.

An ex-Compaq colleague now working for Extreme Networks asked me if I wanted to take on a consulting project to upgrade more than 1,000 Gigabit Ethernet switches at Compaq for $110 an hour during non-prime-time hours. This would keep me out of the

Houston traffic, and as I was so bored, I accepted it. Since I had to create a corporate entity like a limited liability company (LLC) in the State of Texas to start working as an independent consultant, I thought I might as well try to get some local customers here in Brenham. (This idea had first been suggested to me by our local vet while he took care of our just-born colt back in early 1999. The doctor said there was a lot of business potential in Washington County and many small businesses needed computer support. I blew him off since I was still recovering from industry burnout, but that recommendation did echo in my head.)

And so I started Deans Consulting, LLC, and have never looked back. Getting new local clients was slow at first but this eventually gained momentum as the years went by and my reputation grew — as it can in small towns, one way or the other — quickly.

I had only two Brenham clients in 2000, but that increased to five by 2001, 12 by 2002, 25 by 2003, and by mid-2004 I had more than 50 rural customers. I had to stop taking on new clients due to a booked billable calendar until mid-2005.

This business niche in the IT industry that's here in the country has made my life very enjoyable. I look forward to going to work at my client sites every day. They greet me with a smile and are glad to see me. Being in my early forties, I can see myself doing this work for another 20 years since it is so satisfying, low stress, and financially rewarding.

What we need to find out now is if being a rural computer consultant is for you.

What It Takes to Become a Rural Computer Consultant

First of all, you need to have a decent amount of computer support experience or skill sets to be able to hit the ground running. As we will explore in depth later, the recommended (if not required) basic skills are in desktop and server support, with a good knowledge of computer networking. If you are specifically a programmer or even a highly paid Cisco certified networking guru, you still need to be the jack-of-all-computer-trades and have a healthy working knowledge of many computer industry services, for instance, website authoring, upgrading PCs, installing and managing MS Windows, and other PC-related day-to-day activities.

Below is a list of just some of the skills that are required:

- Desktop support (both hardware and software)
- Server support (both hardware and software)
- Network printers and plotters
- Hubs, switches, routers, and firewalls
- Fiber and copper cabling for both data and voice
- Windows installations, tune-ups, troubleshooting, optimization, upgrades
- PDA and cell phone integration
- Website design, migration, and management
- Data-backup configuration and management

Additionally, here is a short list of the higher-level services that a successful consultant working in rural areas would want to provide:

- Project management for large IT build-outs, moves, upgrades, or migrations

- Computer security audits

- Network health studies

- Request for Proposal (RFP) development and management

This sounds like a very wide skill set, and it is. I wrote this book to give a realistic presentation of the requirements for having a successful and profitable rural computer consulting practice, and real skills are required. It is not for the faint of heart or for someone who has held just one or two narrow job roles in the vast world of IT. I would not recommend this for anyone with less than seven or eight years in the external support world.

What I mean by external support is billing your time to multiple clients for computer service, support, or consulting. Internal support is what I did from 1981 to 1991 with CDC and CogniSeis. It was not until mid-1991, when I joined Paranet and they were billing me out to clients at a high hourly rate to perform specific tasks or complete defined projects, that I was performing external support.

The external IT world is much different than the internal IT world, trust me. Every new project is usually a new client and it is very much like going through a job interview and then being put into a high-stress and high-expectation position the next day. After a few years of this, one learns how to adapt to new environments quickly, strategically interface with different client personalities, and complete challenging projects with hard problems in a timely manner. These external support experiences are critical assets for a successful career as a rural computer consultant. So if you are mono-talented in a narrow computer field, you may want to hold off on becoming an independent consultant in a rural area.

In this book I will list in detail the technical skill sets required to profitably service your rural clients. The majority of these skills will not require expensive certifications or costly training, since most can be picked up by reading the right books and taking cost-effective online courses. Some of the skill sets required for this multifaceted position were not in my résumé when I started up in 2000, but just as I had done for nearly 20 years, I taught myself quickly, via computer-based training, which had become much more advanced since those late nights in front of the Plato terminal at Control Data in Houston.

With online tutorials and Internet-based training courses, I was able to pick up numerous tips and tricks, as well as the more complex skills I needed such as web page design and programming. So even if your skill set is more limited at this time, this book can help you prepare for a later shot at becoming a rural computer consultant.

Another factor is money. If you and your spouse are riding high on a $175,000-plus income and have the bills to go along with it (such as a big mortgage, car loans, and other debts), this income would be hard to replace quickly or easily as a rural computer consultant. I do, however, explain later on in this book how to trim down your lifestyle, consumption, and debt to be less dependent on such high salaries.

Your success as a rural computer consultant will be strongly influenced by your customer service skills and attitude. Prompt and friendly customer service is an absolute requirement for small-town business needs. One of the first things I learned was that my new clients strongly desired fast, consistent response. They were tired of waiting for their previous Houston-based computer support person to call back, or better yet, to finally show up on-site to fix the critical computer problem stopping their small but important business task.

You have also got to want to get in front of people, market yourself, sell your services, and adapt to the customs, dialect, and culture of the town's people. If you're a male liberal hippy with tattoos, earrings, and a DNC sticker on your VW Bug, don't count on landing new clients in conservative central Texas near where I live.

The opposite is true for a right-wing, gun-toting conservative like myself trying to get clients in small left-wing towns within Marin County just outside of San Francisco. That said, remember that the majority of small towns are more conservative than liberal, and this is especially true in rural farming and ranching areas. Political leanings will be an issue in small towns, and we will discuss this aspect of client relations in more detail later in the book.

The major potential showstopper to becoming a rural computer consultant is that you and your spouse (if applicable) have got to want to live, work, shop, and raise your kids in a small town. As I explained, this was initially a major issue with my wife. It was rough on her for the first couple of years, due to the vast change in distance to her family and the major change of going to a new church and developing a new set of friends.

If you and your family are addicted to the conveniences of city life, then maybe working in a small rural town will not be for you. But you should check things out by visiting small towns and spending some weekends at bed-and-breakfast inns, which will allow you to meet locals and get the feel of the area.

So if you have the urge to escape the urban rat race, possess a varied computer support skill set, have moderate income needs and debt, and like working directly with clients, you may strongly consider becoming a rural computer consultant.

PART 2

SERVICE NEEDS AND SKILL SET REQUIREMENTS

Growing Your Skills: Key Skill Sets

To succeed as a rural computer consultant, you have to be able to offer a wide variety of services to your clients. You'll be faced with all kinds of situations and will have to solve all sorts of problems effectively. You'll almost certainly need some skills you don't have right now. The good news is that with some effort, you can develop the skills you'll need to serve your rural clients.

Back in my Paranet days, we encouraged our billable consultants to continuously grow their IT skill sets. We paid generously for training, seminars, books, and course materials to help our employees attain certifications and gain new billable talents. This enabled us to place them at clients more quickly and keep them out of the non-revenue-generating category — what we called "the bench."

If we had a Novell engineer sitting for weeks between projects, we lost money on him because Paranet paid full-time salaries and benefits whether or not our consultants were billing. As you computer-industry people already know, expertise needs in the technology field change yearly, if not monthly. Back in Paranet's early days, we had mostly Unix guys, until desktop- and server-support needs came on strong. A couple of years later, the Novell market was hot, which then gave way to the Microsoft market. Towards the end of the 1990s, we were looking for database programmers and administrators (DBAs).

We learned that we had to be ahead of the market curve to be able to provide talent to our clients as their technology needs changed, migrated, and increased. We constantly looked for new hires possessing multiple, wide-ranging skills who could be placed easily and quickly at the first opening that fit their talent profile. Your overall position and stature in the company could be greatly affected by your utilization rate. No one wanted to sit "on the bench" at any of the Paranet offices because that made you underutilized — and therefore effectively unemployed.

While our consultants were on the bench, they were either tooling up for the next contract that was due to start soon or they were taking online courses in something other than what was already in their résumés. We had Unix guys learning Novell, and Novell guys learning Microsoft server administration. Our networking people were picking up programming, and all of us were learning project management. The more we knew how to do and could bill for, the more quickly we were placed with clients. This decreased our bench time and increased our utilization, which in turned grew the company's profits.

This same skill-set growth mentality, which grew Paranet from a one-office, eight-person company in 1991 to a 23-office, 2,000-person company by 1997, can be used by you as a rural computer consultant. The wider the variety of IT services you can provide to commercial clients, the easier it will be for you to land those first few projects and have recurring business from these clients, who, of course, will be in need of your numerous services. In other words, the more services you can provide to this rural market, the quicker you'll build your client list. The busier you are, the more money your consultancy will earn.

Now let's talk about the specific list of IT services that have worked well for me over the years. I've identified 40 skill sets that I provide to my clients, and have organized them into five categories, according to the need my clients have for them.

Sample 1, Rural IT Skill Sets, sorts by demand level the services I have been delivering to my rural small-town clients for the past six years:

5 = Very high demand

4 = Strong demand

3 = Moderate demand

2 = Occasionally required

1 = Rarely required

And you'll find most businesspeople in your new small town will fall into one of the following four categories:

- **Category one**: They want to focus on their core business and want a professional to handle computer issues entirely. This category is the most profitable.

- **Category two**: They want you to assist and work side by side with them to address and resolve IT issues.

- **Category three**: They want to perform the computer tasks themselves and want you to train them by providing the knowledge and technical expertise.

- **Category four**: They already possess the knowledge and experience to handle all computer issues themselves — rare and unprofitable for a consultant.

Sample 1 is a menu of services that can be delivered to clients who fall into categories one, two, and three.

We'll briefly go through each of these 40 services and see which ones you are currently able to offer your potential rural clients, and which ones you'll need to get some training and experience in before implementing them out in the field.

The rest of this chapter focuses on the very high demand, strong demand, and

RURAL IT SERVICE

Very high demand (5):

Desktop support and Windows troubleshooting

Sales, configuration, and management of antivirus systems

Data-backup management

Antispyware configuration and management

PC hardware/software upgrades

Strong demand (4):

Windows server support

Windows software updates

Software sales and installations

Printer configurations and support

ISP selection and configuration

Router configurations and troubleshooting

Website authoring

Website/E-mail hosting

Website/E-mail management

Wireless configurations

Moderate demand (3):

Remote-access configurations

Hardware sales and installations

Client/Server performance troubleshooting

Application support (QuickBooks, etc.)

Hardware/software scaling and purchasing

Hardware/software eBay brokering

Minor network cabling

Network infrastructure troubleshooting

Website promotion

Data recovery services

Occasionally required (2):

VPN solution consulting and configurations

Network design consulting

Network management configurations

Network buildouts and configurations

Smartphone and PDA support

User training

Covert user monitoring

Digital camera and scanner configurations

Digital surveillance projects

Computer security reviews and audits

Rarely required (1):

Light programming in Excel, Access, scripts

Network performance reviews and studies

RFP compilation and management

VoIP consulting and configuration

GPS configurations for asset/expenses tracking

moderate demand skill sets. Chapter 5 continues with a look at occasionally required and rarely required skill sets.

Very High Demand Skill Sets

These are the top five skill sets you'll need to have in rural communities. More than half of my billable time comprises a combination of the following five services, so if you're serious about becoming a rural computer consultant, make sure you have these skills.

Desktop support and Windows troubleshooting

Microsoft Windows–based desktop support service tops the list of very high demand skills. Back in the 1990s when I was building large, 1,000-user campus networks, I had too big an ego to ever think that ten years later I'd be doing desktop support by choice. And I never thought I'd be making better money and actually enjoying it. But it is amazing how your outlook and attitude change when your work environment is positive, cheerful, and low stress — as it can be in rural areas.

I attained the majority of my current client base by solving the problems that got them to contact me in the first place. Those first calls usually had something to do with troubleshooting a Microsoft Windows problem. Windows problems specifically, and desktop support in general, comprise about half of my income, and time at client sites is usually spent dealing with PCs configured with Windows 98SE, Windows ME, Windows NT, Windows 2000, and Windows XP (both Home and Professional).

There are vast online and hard-copy resources for training in these operating systems, and most IT professionals out there already have this one down, just from dealing with their own computers at work and home.

Antivirus software sales, configuration, and management

Computer viruses are here to stay and will continue to wreak havoc on computer users. You would be surprised how many ill-configured, outdated, expired, or even non-existent copies of antivirus programs are out there in the SOHO (small office/home office) environments. The major computer makers started pre-installing 30- or 60-day trial versions of Norton and McAfee antivirus solutions on their computers, but a large majority of them expire and are dysfunctional a few months after the new PC is deployed.

You can bill for the time you spend installing, configuring, verifying, and updating the software, as well as for the software itself. If you buy it from wholesale sources, you can resell it to your client at a profit. After you have resolved all the antivirus software installation and configuration issues, you can run scans on all PCs and oversee the thorough removal of any existing virus infections. Next, you can occasionally schedule a maintenance visit to verify that all virus-definition subscriptions are current, all updates are occurring normally, and scans are being run routinely.

Data-backup management

Managing your client's data backups is the most important task you can perform. There are many ways user files can be lost or corrupted due to user error, hardware failure, theft, or fire. Once you get in a client's door, inquire how they perform backups, if at all. If they are not performing data backups, immediately and strongly propose a tape backup solution for any data farms of more than two gigabytes, or DVD/RWs or other smaller media for less data.

Get them on a daily full-backup process and have it documented either manually by the person who changes the media (such as tapes), or electronically via e-mailed log files. For a second layer of protection, you can utilize online backups, such as those from Intuit, or my favorite, Data Deposit Box, which offers very affordable and secure online, automated, and off-site data-storage services (see www.DataDepositBox.com).

Once you have completed the data-backup project or verified that your client's existing procedure is adequate and working properly, you can offer to monitor the back-up results on a regular basis. I remotely monitor more than a dozen of my clients via e-mailed logs and by checking the backup status on their Data Deposit Box sub-accounts, which I configure under my mail account. I provide this service free of charge for my clients, and I only bill them when I have to take action to resolve any backup problems such as tape errors, file-system modifications, or client backup-duty neglect.

Again, let me stress how critical it is to fulfill this responsibility to protect your clients' data — no matter how lazy they are or ill-equipped the hardware configuration. If their backup procedures are deficient or absent, you need to strongly lobby your clients to implement solid and reliable back-up solutions immediately.

Antispyware configuration and management

Due to the security vulnerabilities in Microsoft's Internet Explorer (IE) (the most used Internet browser in the world), spyware authors have gone wild, creating adware, spyware, and keyloggers to invade our privacy and even steal our identities. A 2004 joint report from EarthLink and Webroot reported that nine out of ten computers connected to the Internet had some level of spyware infestation. Since that equates to 90 percent of your clients having possible computer performance problems due to spyware, there is an incredible business opportunity to help your clients clean up spyware-related issues.

There are good commercial spyware-removal tools (e.g., Spy Sweeper from Webroot.com) built into some antivirus software, such as the most recent version of Norton. My favorite solutions, however, are the free antispyware applications Spybot and Microsoft's Windows Defender. Since no spyware-removal program will eliminate 100 percent of all spyware, you should use a combination of tools. MS Windows Defender teamed with Spybot is a winning pair.

Whenever a client complains of slow computer performance or excessive pop-ups, immediately check for spyware infestation. My solution is to first download, install, update, and run Spybot, followed by MS Windows Defender. You can bill your time at the client site for removing the pesky spyware entities with these two handy utilities, which will most likely speed up the client's PC a great deal and help keep it running smoothly. Though it may take multiple passes with both spyware removal tools in safe mode, the time spent properly cleaning out the spyware will be worthwhile.

PC hardware and software upgrades

Upgrades can be a real moneymaker, even with the low cost of new PCs. Many of your clients will have one- to three-year-old computers with strong CPUs, large hard drives, and decent memory capacity but older or outdated operating system (OS) versions. If the hardware is still reliable and not too far out of performance specifications, it is usually worth adding RAM and upgrading the OS to extend the life of the PC for another few years.

During my first five years as a rural computer consultant, I've upgraded close to 100 computers for both commercial and home users with PCs that had at least a 500MHz CPU and capacity for 512MB of RAM. After adding as much RAM as possible, I would then export all user data, format the hard drive, and perform a clean new installation of Windows XP. From there, I would apply all service packs and updates to the OS, reload all required applications such as MS Office, QuickBooks, and any other LEGALLY PURCHASED software the client had for that PC. Finally, I would import the user's data, including all files that were in the My Documents folder — mail addresses and messages, and all other database user data.

This full reload procedure works much better than doing a step upgrade since it does not bring along all the old programs, settings, and problems associated with the older and probably corrupted version of Windows. The process takes about one to two hours of my hands-on time over a period of three to four hours, depending on the amount of user data and number of layered applications. This is why I strongly recommend taking the client PC back to your home office or computer lab, performing the upgrade in the evening, and returning the client's PC the next day.

Performing this upgrade at your home office allows you to load data and programs while doing other things such as spending time with your family (sneaking off once in a while during the evening to load CDs and click Next).

By 2007, the new version of Microsoft Windows (currently named Vista) will be available. Since Microsoft usually understates the hardware requirements for its operating systems, I would strongly recommend that you upgrade some primary components of any platform to support Vista. On Microsoft's website, www.Microsoft.com/ windowsvista, they have a minimum and a premium set of hardware requirements to support the Vista OS. Their premium should be your base minimum. In fact, I would run no less than a 1.4GHz CPU with HT (Hyper-Thread), at least 1GB of RAM, 80GB HDD, and a separate graphics card with 256MB of memory, since Vista is a graphics hog. If you have a strong spare PC, download the Beta version of Vista free from the Microsoft website while still available, install it, and start getting familiar with it. Microsoft Vista upgrades will be a hot service for you to provide starting in 2007.

Strong Demand Skill Sets

The following ten skill sets fall into the "strong demand" category. Demand for these services may comprise 30 percent to 60 percent of your prospective IT projects.

Windows server support

Most of your clients with ten or more work-stations will have a MS Windows server running either Windows Server 2003, Server 2000, or even the older Windows NT 4.0 Server. Servers are just glorified PCs that share out files, provide print services, and maybe act as the company's e-mail server.

I strongly recommend that you take at least a formal Microsoft server-management course, and possibly even complete the Microsoft server-certification process. Doing so would be especially useful if you will be supporting a Microsoft Exchange environment serving multiple physical locations, since that can get quite complicated.

I was able to pick up the basics of server management of NT 4.0 Server, Server 2000, and even Windows Server 2003 just by taking online courses, reading books, and diving into new server implementations (since the risk was low due to the absence of existing data). Tread carefully here with previously installed Active Directory servers: the risk is high if you are not very familiar with managing user data and accounts.

For workgroup environments with fewer than ten PCs and no formal Domain Controller or Active Directory servers, a properly configured PC can be designated to act as a workgroup server to provide shared files and directories for central data storage and backups. These are much easier to configure and manage than a formal server. If clients cannot afford the high software cost of a formal server, these workgroup server solutions may suit their needs, and you can configure them just by sharing out directories and setting the appropriate file permissions.

Windows software updates

Anyone who has ever used a Microsoft Windows–based PC knows that Windows is in almost constant need of updates from Microsoft. You will be surprised that many PCs both in the work and home environments are far behind in receiving and applying the most recent and required Windows updates. This has improved since automatic updates were enabled by default after Windows XP Service Pack 2 was released and fully implemented, but still, some have chosen to manually disable the automatic update downloads. Larger companies have specifically implemented a nonautomatic Windows-update policy to avoid conflicts with other corporate applications.

I have billed many hours just downloading and applying critical and required Microsoft updates and service packs to both workstations and servers. The big one was in 2004 when XP Service Pack 2 was released. I put the complete 240MB service pack on a CD-ROM and took it from client to client and properly installed it, after making sure the PC had ample disk space and was free of viruses and spyware.

Keep in mind that Microsoft Windows has been and most probably always will be buggy and vulnerable to holes in the code. This can allow worms, Trojan horses, and hackers to penetrate the OS, and it is up to you to make sure your client is protected. Applying the latest and greatest Windows updates and service packs is the best way to shore up a client's operating system.

Software sales and installations

As we talked about in the section on hardware and software upgrades, I have made good money by buying retail, sealed-in-the-box legal versions of Windows and MS Office from online discount software dealers and then selling them to clients at just under retail-store prices. For instance, after registering with Microsoft as a "System Reconditioner," I was able to legally purchase Original Equipment Manufacturer (OEM) versions of their software from online vendors as long as I added hardware value to the PC by adding RAM, which was usually required anyway.

Your profit margin can be widened if you want to take the risk of purchasing new sealed software on eBay. It can be hit or miss, but if you get familiar with the verbiage and pay attention to the seller ratings, you can get good deals. Sometimes you can find brand-new, factory-sealed (in the plastic tubs) versions of Microsoft Windows and Office at half the price they are listed for on the shelves of Best Buy.

After you have purchased the new LEGAL version of the necessary software for the client, do not get greedy and mark it way up. A good rule of thumb is to put it about 5 percent to 10 percent less than the best storefront price from places such as Best Buy or other local large electronic chains and superstores. You can now bill the time it takes to properly install the software as a new installation or as an upgrade to a previous version.

Printer configurations and support

Few things can be more frustrating in our IT world than fighting printer problems. Printers are a pain, but in some small-business environments they are critical, and we can bill time for keeping them running smoothly and printing reliably. Many desktop printers today are throwaways — inexpensive to purchase but very expensive to buy ink cartridges for, so they need to be set up correctly when first installed.

You can also help by sharing out other users' printers within workgroups, so everyone can have multiple printing choices. The three-in-one multifunction printers that scan, fax, and print can be a bit complicated — particularly Hewlett-Packard models — when numerous drivers are running on a Windows PC. If these multifunction printing centers are not configured properly during the installation, all types of printing and computer performance problems may develop.

The higher-grade network-enabled laser printers require expertise to allow a group of network-connected PC users to print to them over the local area network (LAN). For server-based small-company networks, it is a good idea to install the printer and driver on the server, and then share out the network-based printer from the server, which eliminates the need to manually install the driver from CD-ROM on each PC.

Regardless of whether the printer is locally connected or network based, printers need attention, and small-town clients are willing to pay for technical assistance.

ISP selection and configuration

I have yet to visit a business in a small rural town that did not have Internet access for employee usage. In fact, most of my clients are dependent on the Internet for one or more aspects of their job. As rural computer consultants, we have the job of helping our clients choose the Internet service provider (ISP) solutions that best suit their needs based on reliability, bandwidth, and cost.

I am constantly plugged into high-speed ISP choices in my clients' areas, whether it is DSL in town, cable service areas, wireless coverage zones, ISDN for those hard-to-reach locations near town, or finally satellite for those isolated cases. Rarely do I spec out T1 circuits in small towns due to their high cost. The vast majority of my corporate clients have either DSL from the local phone company or a land-based wireless service from the area wireless broadband providers that are common in rural areas.

As a computer consultant, you need to be familiar with all ISP choices, their support characteristics, and the vendor equipment. (For example, I provide the initial setup for DSL connections for 20 percent less than the phone company's installation charge.) You will also be called in to troubleshoot connection problems, verify upstream and downstream throughput, and assist clients with Internet connection security issues.

Router configurations and troubleshooting

My small-company clients connecting to the Internet via DSL, cable TV, wireless, T1, or even ISDN all have routers. The vast majority of the SOHO (small office/home office) routers are made by Linksys, D-Link, Netopia, SonicWALL, or Cisco. Though Cisco routers rule the world, they are actually rarely found at small-town client sites except for those few T1 sites. Since most of the routers are web GUI (graphical user interface) based, the configuration and management is quite easy once you understand the basics of TCP/IP.

Make sure you have a good understanding of how PPPoE (point-to-point protocol over Ethernet) works to connect to the DSL ISPs, and how DHCP (Dynamic Host Configuration Protocol) servers are configured to hand out IP addresses to the DHCP clients receiving those addresses. Since most DSL self-install packages from the local phone company require an initial setup on one PC, I use one of my spare Windows XP laptops to do the start-up. This creates the DSL account and configures the DSL modem that was shipped with the kit. From there, you use that username and password to bring up the new DSL connection on the new SOHO router you are configuring.

Another good thing to do is to keep a spare D-Link and Linksys router in your vehicle to replace broken ones in a flash when you get calls from your clients, especially after thunderstorms, which can take a toll on DSL routers. Buy them cheaply online, and you can make a fair profit on the hardware along with your billable time to configure it.

Website authoring

Back in late 1999, when I started Deans Consulting, LLC, I needed a website to help get my name out there in our new community and to attract prospective clients. Since I had time on my hands back then, I decided to buy Microsoft FrontPage and learn how to write websites.

I used FrontPage's templates and was able to get an initial version of my website up on www.LanWanDesign.com, which was my original domain name since DeansConsulting.com was not available back then. A few years later, I was able to snag that domain name and got better at authoring websites by reading books, viewing other sites' HTML code, and downloading free DHTML and Java Scripts from website authoring sites such as www.DynamicDrive.com.

Once you land a client, successfully perform some IT services, and receive a few payments, you will start getting all sorts of requests from that client that span the range of these SOHO skill sets we are now covering. Sooner or later, your client will ask if you "do websites." Since we rural computer consultants are jacks-of-all-IT-trades, we say "YES!"

Since most websites are simply online brochures and FrontPage is a WYSIWYG (what you see is what you get) HTML editor, creating websites for your clients is not that difficult. You can bill for helping them choose and secure a domain name from the discount provider GoDaddy.com, and assist them in selecting a layout and look by viewing their competitors' websites.

Website and e-mail hosting

Once you are literally forced into becoming a website writer, your next new role will be as webmaster and provider for website and e-mail hosting. Since you need to have somewhere to put your clients' websites, you might as well make money on it and have complete control. Originally, I used the Texas-based EV1Servers.net, which provided virtual websites for $10 a month billed directly to the clients, but they had a major problem in 2004 that left me with a bad taste in my mouth.

Since then, I've contracted out a reseller's account from Webolocity.com, owned now by Beachcomber, which for $25 a month, paid quarterly, gives me 2GB of website storage and 3GB of bandwidth to distribute to the 20 websites I am now supporting. All of my clients' websites (which I either authored or imported from their original hosting locations) now reside on my Webolocity reseller

master account under subaccounts to which I have full administrative access. For each of the client websites I host through this outsourced service, I bill the customer $15 per month — and that adds up quickly when you multiply times 20.

Webolocity's management interface is simple, fast, and very comprehensive. It allows me to provide upstream virus and spam filtering and tagging on unlimited e-mail addresses, along with website access statistics. The main issue here for website and e-mail hosting is easy access, total control, and cost-effective outsourcing that allows you to make monthly income from your client's websites.

Website and e-mail management

Now that you are authoring and hosting websites, you must also do the day-to-day management of keeping the website's content fresh and e-mail addresses up to date. Bill your time while making changes to the client websites, adding e-mail addresses, or performing basic site-management functions.

Since you are parceling out online website storage from your reseller account into smaller chunks for your clients, you may have to adjust quotas, clean out spam boxes, and monitor e-mail box sizes. At your clients' office locations, you will also have the duties of configuring Outlook and Outlook Express e-mail accounts to send and receive e-mail from the websites you manage. All this time is billable to clients at the same rate, whether you are standing at their company PC or sitting in your leather chair working on your wireless laptop at your country home.

I toyed with the idea of setting up my own web server at my ranch to provide website and e-mail hosting services, but once I considered the AC power issues, upstream bandwidth requirements, hardware and software costs, and licensing issues, I decided against it. It is just so much easier and much more profitable to pay Webolocity $75 every three months for plenty of web resources and great online chat-based support.

Wireless configurations

Back in 2000, my buddies at Houston's Compaq Computer (now Hewlett-Packard) were busy installing 802.11b access points (APs), which ran at 11Mb/s. Just a few short years later, I'm just as busy installing the newer 802.11g APs, which run at a snappy 54Mb/s. Somewhere around early 2004, 802.11b/g wireless network interfaces were factory installed by default in the majority of laptops, and the need for wireless zones in my clients' offices and homes has just skyrocketed.

Here is another profit opportunity. Purchase the APs and WNICs (wireless network interface cards) from discount online dealers ahead of time, and sell them to your clients at a modest markup. Since all wireless APs and routers are configured with WEP (wired equivalent privacy) security turned off, your first duty is to enable the 128-bit encryption on the AP and all authorized WNICs for that client. If there is a need for multiple wireless zones and therefore multiple APs, you will need to do a thorough wireless site survey using the exact make and model AP and WNIC that will be ultimately implemented.

After the wireless router or set of wireless APs are installed, configured, and secured, you then need to test both the connectivity signal strength along with throughput in both directions. This can be done using the free tool Qcheck, which is included in my network toolbox. (Look on the accompanying CD-ROM in the toolbox section for a web link, or go to the toolbox on my website at www.DeansConsulting.com.) Wireless configuration projects are good revenue generators since there are multiple phases such as the planning, purchasing, installing, configuring, testing, and finally documenting, which are all billable tasks.

Moderate Demand Skill Sets

The following ten capabilities of a rural computer consultant are in the Moderate Demand category. The combination of these skill sets may comprise 20 percent to 40 percent of your prospective IT projects.

Remote-access configurations

Weren't computers supposed to save us time at work and enable us to work less? We are all working harder and longer at the office, and with remote-access capabilities and high-speed Internet connections, we're working from home as well. The good thing is that if your clients have to put in extra work hours, you can make it possible to do it from their homes by enabling them to connect their home computers to the office systems.

Things have moved on from the days of dial-up modems and pcAnywhere, because now we can connect to the office computer over the Internet using online remote-access services such as GoToMyPC.com. You can perform billable consulting with your client by explaining the advantages of remote access, helping them understand the different options, and configuring their remote-access solution.

If your client likes the idea of connecting to their work PC remotely but does not want to pay a monthly fee to GoToMyPC.com, there are other options. For instance, you can configure the remote desktop (RDT) hosting feature on the office PC, modify the office router's IP and port forwarding, and set up the remote Windows XP PC at their home to use the remote desktop client. For non-XP computers, I use the VNC remote access tool from RealVNC.com. VNC is free, but it takes a little more router configuration.

For multiple remote PCs to access multiple office computers, the host office computers will need their RDT or VNC default port numbers modified, corresponding router forwarding entries must be configured, and the client's connection address needs to specify those new port numbers. If your client has a larger number of remote workers that require remote sessions to the office, you may then have to look at recommending a Citrix server.

Hardware sales and installations

We would all like to avoid selling and installing computer hardware, but these are often tasks clients ask of a rural computer consultant. I try to keep the common, small-cost items on hand — things like routers, switches, and UPSs — which enables me to swing right by with a replacement in a client's time of need.

This is a very helpful service to offer to small-town clients because there usually isn't any large computer or electronics store located nearby. Many times on my trips to Houston to visit relatives I'll drop by Micro Center and buy six or more UPSs on sale. I know that within a month, I'll have sold them all to my clients for a moderate profit,

not to mention the billable time spent installing, configuring, and testing the monitoring software that comes with them.

There have been other incidents of clients calling me when their critical or high-use laser printers die, asking me to pick a new one up from either Houston or nearby College Station and immediately put it into service at their site. Clients will pay for fast service like that. Most don't want to spend half a day traveling to a large electronic store and then try to guess which printer to buy when they have a guy like me who knows exactly what to buy, where to buy it quickly, and how much it should cost.

Client/server performance troubleshooting

This is one of those troubleshooting skills that you will want to sharpen up on because there have been many times these opportunities got me into a new client site. After you do the basic marketing in your area, once in a while you will get a panicked call from a small-business owner (who heard your name from one of your existing clients) about a performance problem with a workstation talking to a server.

To troubleshoot problems like these you will need to have a good technical foundation with Windows, PC hardware, and networking, as well as some familiarity with the software having the performance problem. Of course, start with the basics and eliminate the simple things like workstation memory capacity or overconsumption of the CPU, and work your way to the server (last), especially if only one person is having the problem.

You cannot accurately give estimates for how long it will take and how much it will cost to troubleshoot and resolve potentially complex problems like this, so explain to the client that you will put in your best effort and work in good faith to provide competent computer consulting to fix the issue. If you're ambitious like I was in the beginning, you won't charge the client unless you're able to fix the problem. This may burn some of your time, but most likely you will resolve or at least identify the cause of the performance degradation. From there, you can bill your client for the resolution or prepare a SOW (scope of work) analysis, which lays out the resources needed to permanently fix the trouble.

Application support of common programs

The golden rule here is use the same hardware and software as your clients use. Do not have just a Macintosh with only Apple software and expect to support your Windows-based clients at work. You need to use and be familiar with the exact accounting programs that most small businesses use, for example, QuickBooks, Microsoft's Money, and also Intuit's Quicken for the home users you support.

Let's use QuickBooks as a good example of application support for your clients. You will probably utilize QuickBooks for your own consulting business, as I strongly recommend later in this book — not only for your business financials, but also so you will be well versed in how to back up the data, update the program, and upgrade to new versions in the proper and safe sequence. If you lose data on an unbacked-up version of QuickBooks that has been in use for three years at a client site, you are professionally dead. That counts for double in a small town, which means that professionally speaking, you will be dead and buried.

If a client asks your assistance with any database application that you are not familiar with, first read up on it from the software-maker's website, or better yet, see if you can download a trial copy to get some hands-on time with the program. Immediately figure out how to back up or export the data safely before you attempt any program modification, update, upgrade, or troubleshooting of any of the application's settings.

Application support can be dangerous territory, but it can be also very profitable in the long run — and it can get you happy new clients who will become regular clients.

Hardware and software scaling and purchasing

Many times over the past five years, I have received calls from my clients asking questions about what kind of configurations will they need for new PCs, what version of Microsoft Office will include Access, and how much bandwidth their new office will need for connecting to the home office. Here I am doing basic consulting by listening closely to my customers, analyzing their actual needs, researching what hardware and software solutions will work best for them, and then estimating the cost of resources that will be required for implementation.

Even though rural small-town clients may be detached from big cities, their business needs and concerns can be quite similar to those of urban businesses. It can be quite confusing for them to browse the Dell website and start configuring a workstation or especially a server. Here is where we rural computer consultants can be very helpful — by being familiar with all computer manufacturers' websites, knowing how to "spec out" the configuration that will best suit the client's needs, and being able to order that configuration online. We want to make sure they have ample RAM, CPU strength, bus speed, and room to expand capacity for years to come, therefore ensuring that the equipment has a long service life.

I bill for my time when clients ask me to help them purchase a new Dell server from www.Dell.com, because it can be a challenge to get it right the first time. After saving it to my cart, I sometimes have to call Dell's 1-800 sales number to verify that the server configuration I have chosen presents no compatibility problems or shipping delays.

Client software needs also come up when upgrades are announced that may require Windows updates, service packs, or even newer versions. This is another opportunity for billable consulting time to analyze what your clients' short- and long-term software requirements are and make the best recommendation for software types, versions, and revisions.

For instance, clients sometimes ask me which package of Microsoft Office to purchase, since there can be four to six of them available, depending on the release level. They may just need the bare-bones version like Office Basic (which just has Outlook, Excel, and Word); or, at the opposite end of that scale, there is Office Premium (which has all Office products in one package for twice the price).

Hardware and software eBay brokering

I have also had requests from clients to buy them new and used laptops and desktops on eBay, sometimes on their PayPal accounts and other times on mine. When I use their eBay and PayPal accounts, I just bill them for a small amount of my time, whereas when I utilize my own eBay and PayPal accounts (incurring the usual auction risk that goes along with the purchase), I build some profit into the price I bill them for the requested computer.

There are some great deals on eBay, with new computers from Dell, IBM, HP, and other major manufacturers still sealed in the box. Use the search phrases "new" and "sealed" during your inquiries to find those auction items, which have never been opened, licensed, or configured. Also check the shipping cost to verify it is not outrageously high, and, when ordering in the US, make sure it is not from out of the US, to avoid import fees.

A few of my clients have been out of compliance on the MS Office licensing, which usually means they bought several PCs over the years but used one copy of Office 2000 for all of them. Once I explain the legal issues surrounding that practice, they immediately agree to allow me to help them fix the problem. eBay is a great way to purchase legal versions of Office still sealed in the plastic tub for less than half the price charged by retail outlets.

Minor network cabling

Back in 1995, I got my Registered Communications Distribution Designer (RCDD) certification from BICSI (Building Industry Consulting Service International), an organization that is highly respected in the data and voice cabling industry. I used that RCDD knowledge often during the late 1990s while building out large computer networks, but I rarely use it in the small towns as a rural computer consultant. However, from time to time there is a need to make up longer CAT5E UTP patch cables to reach workstations or other network entities that are located far away from an Ethernet wall-outlet connection.

A box containing 1,000 feet of CAT5E UTP cable, a simple RJ-45 crimper tool, and a punch-down tool, costing less than $50 each, along with some CAT5 inserts and connection heads, will allow you to complete the majority of these cabling projects. The inserts that pop into face plates are color coded, and the pin layout for the RJ-45 connection heads can be downloaded from my site at www.DeansConsulting.com on the Toolbox web page.

For larger cabling projects and fiber cabling tasks, find a good data cabling contractor who is willing to drive to your small town on a couple of days' notice to pull and terminate multiple data cables. You can still bill time for project management. If you are willing to pay the cabling contractor from your bank account, you can add your markup and then bill the client along with your time.

Network infrastructure troubleshooting

If you come across a network connectivity or performance problem and you have ruled out problems with the computers themselves, it's time to troubleshoot the networking infrastructure. This will include the network cabling (whether copper or fiber) and how those cables are terminated, routed, and patched. Also included are the passive (nonpowered) and active (powered) connection devices such as patch panels, couplers, hubs, switches, routers, and firewalls.

One of the best and most comprehensive resources for learning and understanding computer networking can be found in the Network Design Reference Manual (NDRM), which can be purchased from www.bicsi.org. You can use this manual as a guidebook to help you learn the standards and metrics of every kind of computer networking entity currently and previously in use on large and small networks.

You will need some basic troubleshooting tools, such as a UTP cable pair tester to verify you have connectivity for your Ethernet cabling. In my experience patch cables are notorious for being the problem, and after that it is usually the terminations of the CAT5E UTP cabling. Next, look for pinches or harsh crimps in the cabling along with new sources of EMI (electromagnetic interference). If you get a call that the network is having problems after a thunderstorm, immediately look for blown hubs or switches due to electrical spikes from direct or even nearby lightning strikes.

This type of troubleshooting is hard to learn, but can be a very valuable skill set to possess and can get you in the door when a new client calls, asking you to come fix a networking problem.

Website promotion

Promoting a website, whether it is one you have authored, one you host, or one you have little to do with, is a consulting service you can provide to your clients to help them increase the legitimate traffic to their websites. The key word here is "legitimate," because there are many unscrupulous services out there that can generate a large amount of bogus hits that are really driven by pay-for-surf sister companies of the website-promotion organization.

First you will want to review your client's meta tags for proper key words and phrases, so the web spiders and search engines will pick them up properly. There are several free meta-tag analyzing websites on the Internet to help you tune up key word and description tags (for example, try www.widexl.com, which will give you all sorts of recommendations).

My favorite way to promote a website is to use the pay-per-click service of Google's AdWords. All you need to do is set up an AdWords account with Google under a credit card and then configure an ad that appears in the "Sponsored Links" section on the right side of the Google results page. The AdWords service allows you to set a daily budget with a minimum of $1 per day. The more click-throughs you get per impression rate, the cheaper the per-visitor rate, with it averaging around $0.15 each. Google also has great report generation, allowing you to see how much your ad is being viewed and how many visitors are being drawn to your site due to the AdWords campaign.

If you are hosting the client website through the Webolocity hosting service, you can utilize one or more of the website statistic tools under the cPanel application suite. You can bill your time for efforts to increase the visitor count to your client's website, and prove it by creating reports from both Google's AdWords reporter and Webolocity's website statistical utilities.

Data recovery services

I have had some very tough country cowboys in my town call me, almost in tears, begging me to come over right away to their office or home and get their data back from a troubled hard drive, damaged tape, or corrupted floppy. No matter how much I preach and teach how incredibly important it is to perform backups, clients still get themselves into a bind and will lose data from time to time — and you can make a hefty profit by salvaging it for them.

First of all, if the client is one you're already serving, YOU BETTER HAVE THAT DATA BACKED UP YOURSELF! Then all you have to do is restore it from last night's tape backup or download it from Data Deposit Box, like I've already recommended.

However, if it's a new client or one of those with whom you have only spotty contact, it's your job to do everything you can to recover the lost data. The best tool I have found is called GetDataBack from www.Runtime.org, which, for US$119, offers a twin-pack tool set for both FAT and NTFS file systems. Buy this software utility as soon as you can, get familiar with how it works, and try it out on an older hard drive. You will make twice or even three times your original investment on your first recovery project.

Since it may take quite an effort to remove the client's hard drive, place it in your own test PC, and run the many passes it may take to recover the data, the billable time will add up fast. Set a minimum attempt fee of at least one hour of billable time, and if you successfully retrieve the client's data, charge them for all the time you put into the effort. Trust me: they'll be so happy that even a large bill from you won't break their smile.

The skill sets described in this chapter will probably account for as much as 70 percent of your business. But that doesn't mean you can relax and stop there. There are other services your clients will require from you, and to really be successful as a rural computer consultant, you'll need to provide them. Those skill sets are the subject of Chapter 5.

5

Growing Your Skills:
Less Frequently Required Skill Sets

The skills sets discussed in this chapter aren't requested by clients as often as those discussed in Chapter 4. Nonetheless, they'll make up a substantial part of your business. If you don't already have these skills in your toolbox, there's no time like the present to start acquiring them.

Occasionally Required Skill Sets

The following ten capabilities of a rural computer consultant come under the Occasionally Required category. The combination of these skill sets may comprise from 10 percent to as much as 25 percent of your prospective IT projects. Therefore, it's worth your while to master as many of them as possible.

VPN solution consulting and configurations

Virtual private networks (VPNs) are more common now that uncomplicated and affordable solutions are available from SOHO router makers such as Linksys (which is owned by Cisco Systems). Just for review, a VPN can allow two geographically separated company offices to "see" each other as one logical network across the Internet. This is done via software, or a router and software combination, or just two VPN routers as endpoints.

A properly working VPN can allow a client to have one server providing data services to both a local and a remote office via the Internet. As far as users are concerned, the shared folders, networked printers, and e-mail services from servers on the far side of a VPN link are indistinguishable (though they may actually be a bit slower) from file shares and printers on the local side.

Your job as a rural computer consultant is to help the client plan, purchase, configure, test, and implement the VPN for reliable and robust data service between the two office locations. The trick here is to make sure the ISPs at each site provide enough upstream bandwidth, especially from the server side of the VPN. A standard 128Kb/s ADSL link from the local office housing the server most likely will not be sufficient.

My favorite VPN configuration is a pair of identical BEF41VP VPN endpoint routers from Linksys, which cost less than $100 each. The VPN configuration is simple and stable, and using hardware endpoints eliminates the installation and management of VPN client software on the server — or worse, on each one of the client workstations at the remote site. Customers rarely want to tackle this project without professional help, so your billable time is critically needed here, even though this service is only occasionally requested.

Network design consulting

You will eventually be called in on a project to design a new computer network for either an office remodel or an entirely new office layout. This is when the Network Design Reference Manual (NDRM) mentioned in Chapter 4 (which can be purchased from www.bicsi.org) will be absolutely critical. This manual is not cheap, but you will easily earn its purchase price back on the first project.

The big issue in this kind of work is making sure you draw out a new network design map that shows the data cabling origin — which is called the MDF (main distribution frame) — and how the cables are routed to each of the user locations or work areas (WAs). For new buildouts, I strongly recommend that you run two UTP CAT5, CAT5E, or CAT6 cables to each office or WA to connect a PC and possibly a second device, such as a network printer.

One of your network design deliverables to the client will be PowerPoint drawings of the new cabling infrastructure detailing the connections to patch panels and wall jacks along with all required interconnections between the Ethernet switches for the local area network (LAN) and the router for the Internet. (Make sure you do it in PowerPoint, since more Windows PCs can view Power-Point files than other formats such as Visio.) Another deliverable will be an Excel spreadsheet with costing estimates for cabling, network hardware, installation labor, configuration, and testing. Review the design and numbers first with another IT consultant you know and have him or her critique it for errors and omissions. Later, present your network design deliverables to the client along with your plan for project management of the complete network buildout.

Network management configurations

Your larger clients — ones with 10 to 50 employees running moderate-size networks, with a server, numerous workstations, and networked printers — will most likely need some form of network management. Your first step in this situation is to create (or update) a network map in PowerPoint that displays all network devices, including switches, hubs, routers, firewalls, and cabling interconnections, and printed on a single large sheet of paper.

I have created network maps for clients with more than 500 routers and switches on a single sheet of ANSI-E-size (that's 34" x 44") plotter paper. Most of the network maps you'll do for your small-town clients will fit on a tabloid-size sheet of 11" x 17" just fine, although 13" x 19" would be ideal.

After you have completed your map, you'll propose a network management system. This is simply a dedicated PC that will run an SNMP (simple network management protocol) application to ping all devices on the company's network every 60 seconds and that will e-mail or page the appropriate personnel (preferably you) if any critical component, such as a server, goes down. My favorite is WhatsUp Professional by Ipswitch. It is very easy to use and can handle anything from small networks all the way up to large LANs with thousands of nodes.

Another good tool for measuring network performance of a LAN or Internet connection is the application PRTG from www.Paessler.com. This handy statistics monitoring and graphing tool displays the incoming and outgoing rates from any SNMP interface on Ethernet switches and routers. Also included in this tool is a built-in web server to distribute the graphs to remote workstations on the network. The freeware editions will cost you nothing if you only need one or two interfaces for personal or commercial use. You will need to purchase the commercial edition if you are monitoring three or more network interfaces.

Network buildouts and configurations

When clients grow their office areas, open new locations, or even renovate their existing facilities, you will be brought in to consult on cabling and network equipment needs. This will be another time to refer to the Network Design Reference Manual (NDRM) from www.bicsi.org. There are no more Token Ring or other legacy networking technologies being deployed these days, and

best-practice design for Ethernet, the de facto standard, is reasonably cut-and-dried for small offices.

We are still using 10/100Base-TX Ethernet to workstations (which runs at 100Mb/s over UTP CAT5E or CAT6) and then Gigabit Ethernet for connecting switches and LAN routers together. Over the next few years, as Gigabit NICs (network interface cards) and switches become less expensive, the norm will be 10/100/1000Base-TX over UTP for all network connections.

Network connections between buildings should be single-mode fiber optics with at least six strands of fiber in a sheath. Avoid using multi-mode since there are more bandwidth- and distance-expanding capabilities with single-mode fiber. Be aware, however, that unlike multi-mode fiber (which uses an LED), single-mode fiber uses a laser and can cause eye damage or even blindness. At Compaq we had a saying: "Never look into the fiber with your remaining good eye." Do not waste time trying to terminate and test fiber projects yourself. Farm that out to the professionals, since it takes expensive equipment and a great deal of time to learn how to terminate and polish fiber correctly.

Most likely the cabling work will be contracted out to cabling companies, but you can still bill consulting hours by project-managing the buildout. This is critical to make sure the cabling work is executed on a timely basis and follows all the relevant EIA/TIA standards.

Wireless networking will also most likely be required in new network configurations, so stay informed about the latest standardized wireless solutions. At the time this book was written, the 54Mb/s version of the 802.11 standard (called 802.11g) was in full implementation, and the next step up to 300Mb/s (called 802.11n) was being debated by the IEEE (Institute of Electrical and Electronics Engineers) standards committee.

New network buildouts and the inevitable network upgrades are golden opportunities for rural computer consultants to configure rock-solid, robust, and standards-compliant computer networks for their rural clients.

Smartphone and PDA support

I think I was the first geek in Washington County to have a Palm OS Smartphone from Kyocera that could synchronize with Microsoft Outlook on my Windows PC. This mirrored all my 700-plus contacts, tasks, calendar, and notes to and from my smartphone, which doubled as a PDA. Before smartphones were available, I had to carry a cell phone and a Palm OS PDA that stored all my phone numbers, passwords, and a time sheet to track my billable hours during the day. So when the first smartphone from Verizon became available back in 2002, I just had to jump at the chance to carry only one communications and computing device on my belt.

By 2004, smartphones had both improved and gotten cheaper, and when I migrated to the new palmOne Treo 600, my clients took notice. By the next year, I was getting requests from clients to help them combine the phone numbers in their older cell phones with the information in their MS Outlook Contacts to create a single database holding all postal addresses, phone numbers, e-mail addresses, and notes. From there,

I helped them install and configure the synchronization software to mirror their precious data from the PC to their new smartphone.

To avoid accidentally overwriting any data or having massive duplication errors going to and from the smartphone, you must back up the Outlook folders into a PST file *before* you start the smartphone synchronization process. I strongly suggest you purchase and use the latest and greatest smartphone on the market. That way, you'll have experience with it and know the best available software utilities. You may even want to consider having a second phone as a backup and buy a different smartphone brand, such as a BlackBerry or even a Microsoft-based PDA/smartphone.

I favor the Palm OS–based smartphones, but the more smartphone types we're familiar with, the more time we can bill to support these new but soon-to-be-standard communications and computing devices. By the end of this decade, all cell phones will have intelligent capabilities and will serve as both voice and data communications devices, storing critical databases that will need to be backed up daily.

User training

Some rural clients will want your help to learn specific skills to accomplish computer-related projects. I have one client who runs a major automobile dealership who not only loves to tinker around with the workstations, network cameras, and routers, but who also actually understands and fixes the vast majority of IT problems that I handle at other client sites.

Computer-savvy clients like him just need your occasional advice or a visit to help them understand and resolve a complicated problem on which they have already spent a lot of time.

The key to this situation is educational resources. Over the years, I have collected numerous PowerPoint presentations on computer networking, software configuration, hardware troubleshooting, and networking topologies and have had many occasions to present these to clients one on one and even in group settings. These educational tutorials provide vital technical knowledge that my clients can directly apply to their everyday high-tech needs. These tutorials are highly valued, not to mention very billable.

I recommend investing $1,000 in a portable LCD projector that can be attached to your laptop, enabling you to provide educational sessions to your clients.

Another great service that you can provide is help accessing an online training program such as the one I use called Virtual Training Company (www.VTC.com). You can help your client set up an account on this virtual training site, which has hundreds of multimedia courses on networking, Windows, and most applications used in business environments today.

Whether you are actively training your clients, giving tutorials, or showing them how to get online computer-based training sessions, it's all billable time *and* it benefits your client base.

Covert user monitoring

Covert monitoring sounds scary and sordid, but I do get these requests from time to time

at both client office locations and at their homes.

Before you set up any covert monitoring for a client, first check the privacy laws applicable in your jurisdiction, and make sure you operate within the legal limits. Generally, companies have full and complete access to all data residing on and flowing through their corporate networks, and they want to verify there is no excessive personal computer activity or overt negative actions that may jeopardize the company's operation.

For more than ten years now, companies have had to monitor, filter, and fight pornography on their computer networks. When I was at Compaq back in 1998, I heard about the monthly roundup: the network security team would pull the list of the top 20 people attempting to download porn (which was strictly against corporate policy and spelled out explicitly in the employee handbook). This team would meet with the offenders' managers on the last Friday of the month around 2 p.m., and by 3 p.m., those ignorant porn hacks would be out the door forever with all their stuff in a box.

Smaller, rural companies have the same problem, and you will eventually be contacted to help them detect unauthorized website access, illicit e-mail content, or even pornography files already downloaded to the company PCs. There are many software utilities from www.ContentWatch.com and www.IamBigBrother.com that can covertly monitor all user computer activity and verify employees' use of corporate networking facilities.

You will also have the occasional request from an embarrassed client whom you've had for a while and who has gotten to know and trust you, asking you to come to his or her home during lunch and install that same Internet monitoring software on the kids' PCs to verify their web activities. As long as your jurisdiction's laws allow it, help the concerned parent out, but also bill for the time.

Digital camera and scanner configurations

There are few people who still use film cameras these days. Digital cameras are becoming more affordable, easier to use, and provide ever-increasing image quality. Just like PDA smartphones, you need to own at least one digital camera. I have tried to buy new ones every two years and just hand the older ones down to my wife and then to the kids.

Your clients will want your advice on the type, model, and set of features when they're looking for a new digital camera. Since these devices all connect directly to computers via USB or FireWire, you will need to be fully informed on the latest options and capabilities of the latest models. I find websites such as www.dpreview.com most helpful with this. You can also help your clients learn to efficiently manage the ever-increasing image-file sizes and to resize, crop, and compress the BMP and JPG formats.

From there you can advise them on how to safely store and organize the images with programs such as Google's Picasa (www.picasa.com). You can even help them organize their digital photos by simply using MS Explorer. Advise them to create folders with date names, using a standard naming format such as yyyy-mm-dd.

Scanners can be another tricky computer peripheral that users need help with from time to time. Show them how the scanning resolution affects not only the quality of the image, but the file size as well. Many times I have had to reinstall the scanner software due to problems stemming from clients moving the scanner to another PC or upgrading the Windows version of the scanner-connected PC. If they have lost the original installation CD, you can save the day by downloading the appropriate software from the vendor's website and burning it onto a new replacement CD.

Since the images from my clients' digital cameras and scanners are digital computer files, I can play an important role in helping my clients manage them. My billable time can be utilized to verify the digital images are created, transferred, compressed, manipulated, and stored properly.

Digital surveillance projects

With webcams becoming more prevalent and digital cameras becoming more affordable, companies are implementing completely PC-based security systems with digital motion cameras. We can be a part of this business. Again, first check your state or provincial laws to see if you need a license (as we do in Texas) to set up or manage security systems, since there seems to be government involvement (if not unnecessary intrusion) in every aspect of our lives.

State legal and licensing issues aside, there is a good market in rural areas for digital surveillance, in both office and home environments. A surveillance system can be created with a picture-capturing program and a Windows PC with a single USB webcam attached to it. The application I use to watch my backyard is from www.SupervisionCam .com. This awesome and inexpensive program can read digital images from both USB webcams and Ethernet-connected digital motion cameras. You can configure SupervisionCam to just take pictures when motion is detected, which is determined by comparing the differences between adjacent digital picture frames.

My clients have used these digital surveillance systems to monitor their offices, both inside and out. The client that I mentioned previously who runs an auto dealership has close to 20 digital motion cameras watching critical areas all over his operation. Before installing the LAN-connected digital surveillance cameras, he had problems with vandals and thieves stealing and damaging his inventory. After installation, the criminal activity simply vanished.

You can provide consulting and configuration services to your clients by helping them design, purchase, install, configure, tune, and test these affordable and flexible surveillance systems. Though you'll probably be called on only occasionally to provide this service, it can be a profitable one for an experienced rural computer consultant, since the setup and configuration phases of these projects can be quite labor intensive.

Computer security reviews and audits

Every company should be concerned about computer security. We hear numerous stories every week about viruses, worms, and hackers, but there is also the prevalent threat to computer security from sources within the small-company network. When the big security-breach stories hit the news, I can count on at least one call from an existing client (or prospective client) inquiring about having

me perform a study on their computer network to analyze their security effectiveness.

These security reviews and audits are my favorite projects, since I get to play the bad guy without the risk of getting into any real trouble — all while being paid for it. It does take some realistic know-how to be able to aggressively test the security walls protecting computer networks, but there are also very helpful how-to-hack books and websites that will shock you with the abundance of methods they publish. The www .SANS.org site is one of the best sources of information to help you prepare for anything from just a brief computer network security review to a full-fledged and comprehensive security audit.

Microsoft also offers a good tool called the Microsoft Baseline Security Analyzer (MBSA). You can run this tool on a server, and it will produce a great-looking security audit report that you can import directly into your security findings presentation. They also have the Microsoft Security Assessment Tool (MSAT) which provides information and recommendations to enhance security within your IT infrastructure.

To test the external vulnerabilities of a client's network, you can use free online Internet security tools such as ShieldsUP!! from www.GRC.com. For full and thorough Internet vulnerability testing projects, I use the more comprehensive service (for a fee) at www.SecuritySpace.com. It takes almost a day to run its battery of test intrusions, but it then produces a fantastic HTML report that will be a key item in your final security audit report.

Whenever you're hired for a network security review or audit project, at the very least request an e-mail from the client authorizing you to test the security layers of the network, since you will probably be setting off alarms and generating log file entries during your testing efforts. The deliverable should be a wide-ranging report covering all agreed-upon areas of security concern, formatted in HTML and delivered on CD-ROM for the presentation of findings using your projector. Also make sure you have a list of security issue resolution recommendations that addresses all computer network vulnerabilities.

The security study, along with the ensuing projects needed to fix the security problems you find, can help you lock down your client's computer environment and can be very profitable.

Rarely Required Skill Sets

The following five capabilities of the rural computer consultant are in the Rarely Required category. The combination of these skill sets may comprise less than 10 percent of your prospective IT projects. However, it is still important to have these skills since any one of them can get you into a new client's door.

Light programming in Excel, Access, and scripts

Many small businesses have homegrown macros, scripts, and little programs written in MS Access that their company depends on for day-to-day activities. Having a programming or software-support background will be beneficial to you as a rural computer consultant and will open up opportunities to support the kind of small, custom applications I have seen so many of over the years.

There are many books on Amazon and in computer stores that can quickly teach you how to program MS Excel macros, design tables in MS Access, and write simple DOS scripts. The book series that includes *Excel for Dummies* and *Access for Dummies* can help you get started fast or can be used just as a quick reference to troubleshoot a macro problem for a client.

I wrote a simple one-line script in a .BAT file that can be executed nightly by the Windows scheduler. It just copies the "outlook.pst" file from deep inside the file system over to the server to back up a user's Outlook contents. That little one-line script has prevented the loss of hundreds of items in the Contacts folder, not to mention the thousands of e-mails that could have been lost due to hard-drive failures on client workstations.

Another good source you can use to pick up these light-but-profitable programming skills is the virtual-training site www.VTC .com I mentioned earlier. It is well worth the US$30 per month fee to be able to take a quick Access course the night before you need to troubleshoot a table lookup problem at a prospective client's site the next day.

Network performance reviews and studies

While the two main types of studies I have performed at rural small-town companies are security and network-performance related, of the two, it is more likely that you'll get requests for security studies. That said, when network studies do come up, you'll want to jump on them. These are great opportunities to acquire new clients or grow your consulting presence at an existing client's site.

Just as you'd do with a network security review or audit, you'll be looking for problems and provide a written report in HTML format. Describe your findings in detail, then list the prioritized action items to be implemented to resolve the problems. This is just like creating your own billable consulting project list, custom-tailored for that environment. In other words, you'll be getting paid well to inspect the client's network for problems that currently or soon thereafter will impair that network's integrity and performance.

Here is where the expensive network-analysis software tools come in handy. Though costly, the Engineer's Edition Toolset software from www.SolarWinds.net is well worth the investment. This large assortment of SNMP (simple network management protocol) software applications can discover all network entities, monitor them, watch network traffic, and create incredible reports, charts, and graphs for your network performance study report.

You will also want to browse eBay for used laptops in the $500 range to run these network-analysis tools. Usually, you will leave them on client-site networks to gather performance data over a period of one week. Other tools such as WhatsUp Professional from www.Ipswitch.com can also provide good network-analysis applications to help you determine LAN/WAN uptime, utilization, and problem areas.

RFP compilation and management

Requests for Proposals (RFPs) are rare, but when an opportunity arises, it is important that you be prepared and ready to assist your client. Over the years, I have written and executed RFPs for large companies to acquire complete, concise, and accurate proposals from vendors for network cabling, network equipment, computer servers, and workstations. As consultants, we're brought in as vendor-independent, nonbiased third parties to assist clients in creating a document that explicitly describes their project needs and lays out in detail the process of pricing and purchasing the materials and labor required to complete the project.

A good resource to use when preparing RFPs is the www.bicsi.org site, which has presentations and even template RFPs you can download and use as a starting point. Make sure you have a strong understanding of the client's needs and of all aspects of the project so that you can author an understandable and technically accurate RFP document. This document will be one of the deliverables of your service, and it should be easy for the prospective vendors to understand. They should have very few questions if your RFP is properly written.

You can also bill your client for the next phase of the RFP project: managing the RFP process by documenting and answering any vendor questions related to the RFP, and then assisting your client in evaluating the RFP responses. This evaluation should be done on both a monetary and vendor-quality basis to help your client choose the best bid and select the most qualified vendor.

Since your participation comes early in the project, odds are that the client will then ask you to project-manage the computer network buildout or reconfiguration — which means more billable time for your rural consulting business.

VoIP consulting and configuration

Voice over Internet Protocol (VoIP) has been growing rapidly since Vonage jumped onto the scene in 2004 with their funny ad campaign using stupid human stunts on video. Vonage and other companies such as Packet8 offer voice service over the Internet to both business and home users. To take advantage of their service, you must already have a high-speed broadband connection to the Internet. They provide a small device that plugs into your LAN, into which you connect your plain old telephone, and voilà! — you get a dial tone.

Most VoIP plans cost about $20 per month for a large amount of talk time or even unlimited minutes in some cases. Since many of our rural small-town clients have vendors and customers located in other towns and cities, their long-distance bills can take a big chunk out of their bottom line. Consulting with your clients on VoIP solutions can help them save money and also generate revenue for you.

I have shown home users how to download and configure the free VoIP client software from www.Skype.com, which offers voice connections between computer-based phones. They also have a great two-cents-a-minute plan for calling from your computer to an outside analogue POTS (plain old telephone system) line. I use the Skype service in both ways — to talk to my tech buddies via our USB-connected headsets for free and to converse with family members who still use regular phones.

Either way, you can bill your consulting time by configuring these VoIP solutions and managing the bandwidth they consume on the Internet connection, along with monitoring the performance of both the data and voice services that are critical to your clients.

GPS configurations for asset/expenses tracking

Now that we have GPS systems available in most vehicles, along with more affordable handheld GPS devices, I have been getting requests from clients to help them integrate this technology into their daily business and personal lives.

Companies with corporate cars and trucks are especially interested in tracking their vehicles' locations and speed during the business day. For insurance purposes alone, it has become very advantageous for businesses to monitor their mobile assets via GPS. Since most devices and tracking services require computer and Internet interaction, there are numerous consulting opportunities developing in this industry.

You can advise your clients on the GPS tracking service that best suits their needs. You'll do this after you first gather all your customers' tracking requirements, research at least five GPS tracking solutions, and then develop a written recommendation listing the pros and cons of each solution along with reasons for your final choice.

You can offer these same research and setup services to clients who want to monitor their kids' driving. I predict that by late 2006, most cell phone providers like Cingular and Verizon will offer GPS location services over the web for a small monthly fee. An authorized user will be able to log in to the cell provider's website, type in the cell phone number along with a secure PIN, and then see the exact location of the cell phone and its user on a city map onscreen.

Skill Set Wrap-Up

After browsing these 40 services and their required skill sets, you may be a bit overwhelmed. Some of these skill sets, such as Windows Server support, are more comprehensive than others. Windows Server support requires months if not years of experience configuring and managing Windows Server platforms. Since this is such a critical service, you may want to take a formal Microsoft course or even attain an official certification. Other skill sets such as desktop support and Windows management can be picked up quickly by supporting PCs owned by family and friends.

I cannot stress enough the importance of having as many of these skill sets as possible. Service diversity is key to being a rural computer consultant. Set goals for yourself to pick up and learn one new skill set per month to slowly but surely build up your service inventory.

PART 3

PREPARATION

6

Planning Your Move to the Country

If you've decided that rural computer consulting is the life for you, and you've assessed your skills and know you have enough of the 40 skill sets I've just discussed to really make a go of it, you still have a lot of preparation ahead of you. You'll need to get your finances in order not only for starting your new business but also for making a major home move. Most important, you need to be sure you have your family behind you before you take that first step. And that's what we'll look at first in this chapter.

Family Move Issues

If you are unmarried and don't have a significant other, this chapter may not apply to you. However, if you're anything like me — married with a young family and with a child from a previous marriage — this chapter does concern you. In any case, this chapter will likely apply to the majority of us, since by the time we're thinking about leaving the city, odds are we're already raising families.

Moving to a new home is stressful. Changing jobs is stressful. Starting a new business is stressful. Doing all three at once can be horrendous. If you are married with children, becoming a rural computer consultant will be a major challenge, and you'll need to have support from all affected family members, but primarily from your spouse.

I cannot stress this enough: you have got to have 100 percent support for this major life-changing decision. Since many families are dependent on two incomes and have kids in city schools, the issues can get complicated and emotional. You may be lucky and have a spouse who grew up in the country and has always wanted to go back to small-town living. However, you may instead find yourself in the same situation as I did.

My wife did not like the idea of living in the country at first, since she is a city girl and was used to being close to the malls and her mom. She had even been in the habit of choosing jobs based partly on their proximity to her home, so that she wouldn't need to drive on Houston's freeways. Most of us don't have this luxury, but fortunately for her, it sheltered her from the grinding traffic that burns out many of us on a daily basis.

She liked the country place that we bought and approached it with a positive attitude during the whole first year we spent our weekends there. As the year rolled on, I became increasingly frustrated and depressed when we returned to Houston on Sunday nights, and she felt that. We both enjoyed our weekends on the ranch, but I wanted to live up there in peace and quiet full time.

As I described in Chapter 2, I began my lobbying campaign to convince my wife that we should sell our city home and relocate permanently to our ranch. Looking back on it now, I probably acted too fast in selling the house and moving our growing family to the country. So learn from me. Though moving to our ranch was the best thing in the long run for my family — we are doing great now — it's not a good idea to change everything all at once. My poorly timed escape from urban and suburban stresses had, in fact, put unnecessary stress on my wife. The moral of this story is you must make sure the timing of the move is the best possible for all concerned, especially your spouse.

Over the next year or two, Beth adapted to our new home and lifestyle and learned to appreciate the benefits of rural living. She was able to still make the 90-minute drive back into Houston to visit museums, malls, and her family.

If you have kids living with you, the best thing for you to do is to at least wait until the end of the school year, or maybe even until they move from grade school to junior high or high school. Kids will complain no matter where you want to move them. Since we are the parents, pay the bills, and know what is best for them, they will just have to adapt! They're young and they can handle it.

One way to get your family in the mood and mode to dump the city life and take up residence in the country is to have an extended visit with a friend or family member who lives there. Your family needs to spend the night (if not the whole weekend) out in the country and be able to hear only crickets in the evening, see the stars at night, and witness the beautiful sunrise through the trees the next morning.

They need to experience walking down a quiet country road without dodging tricked-out speeding cars. They need to walk around a peaceful pasture and enjoy the wide-open spaces and all the freedoms that go with rural living. Take the opportunity to do some target shooting or even hunting out in the wilderness.

If you don't have any friends or family living rurally, then find a bed-and-breakfast in a small town that looks interesting, and spend the weekend. Walk around the town shops on Saturday and talk to the local people about what it's like to live there. Ask them about the pros and cons, and how long they've been living in that small town. Drive around the rural roads and look at the types of farms, ranches, and nice country homes that enjoy both privacy and solitude in open areas.

Watch the local papers for small-town events and festivals and make plans to attend them. You can mingle with the people of a rural town you're interested in, and you and your family can experience how friendly people are in the country.

You can help build a greater level of comfort for your family by having them experience and gain a better understanding of what they're getting into. This will help move the process along and create support for your idea.

This has to be a family decision, with both Mom and Dad agreeing as one to go ahead with this major change of life for the betterment of the family.

Financial Preparation

Preparing financially for the move to become a rural computer consultant is probably the most difficult task of this life-changing project.

You have to save up enough capital to be able to self-fund this major endeavor. You'll be leaving the corporate environment along with that steady paycheck, selling your existing home, buying another one in a new and strange area, and then starting a new business in which all aspects of success and failure are yours.

Financial planning and preparation is absolutely critical and requires a large amount of discipline, a change of spending habits, and a complete alteration of your urban or suburban lifestyle.

First, let's look at the big picture. What you must do is develop a plan for the following financial tasks during the first critical phases of this project:

Pre-Move Financial Tasks

- Reduction of all forms of existing debt
- Significant saving effort for capital investment

- Massive saving effort for household expenses
- Health insurance evaluation and cost planning
- Scaling back of consumer spending

Post-Move Financial Tasks

- Further cost-cutting efforts to lower monthly fiscal output
- Utilizing lower-cost services and tax exemptions in rural areas
- Strenuous household accounting to stay on budget
- Continuing old-debt reduction and new-debt avoidance
- Running a consulting business on a cash-flow basis

Depending on your current financial situation, the big variables are how long it will take you to prepare financially for the move, and then how tight money will be after the move and during the first few years of your new career as rural computer consultant.

Pre-move financial tasks

The devil of them all in the world of money is debt. Debt is an old monkey on your back that just gets heavier and meaner as time goes by. The debt monkey becomes a major problem when you just throw peanuts to it by making minimum payments on credit-card debts. Your first goal is to kill the debt monkey, just as we do skunks out here in the country.

You need to pay off all credit-card debts, student loans, and even the notes on your vehicles to get ahead enough to start saving and building financial capital for your own consulting business. This may take many months if not years, but it will be worth it in so many ways.

First, pay off all credit-card debts. You might want to consolidate these debts to reduce the overall principal, and then, to knock down the balance, immediately start making large monthly payments in multiples of the minimum payment. Don't even think of resorting to bankruptcy. Bankruptcy will haunt you for years, and will wipe you out in your new small town when word of it gets out.

Next, scale back the monthly cost of your vehicles, since they can send enormous amounts of money down the drain every 30 days. Pay off the remainder of your note on any vehicles less than four years old. Maintain these paid-off vehicles so you can get three to five more years out of them. If you have a brand-new $50,000 Lexus with a $600 monthly note for the next five years, you may want to bail out on it for a $25K Dodge Ram 1500 truck that will serve you much better out in the country.

You may also want to consider refinancing your home mortgage, either with or without "cash-out." Rates have never been lower (as of the time this book went to press), and if you've been in your home a while, you could quite likely benefit substantially from a lower interest rate. The reduction in your monthly payments could be as much as $300. Alternately, if you prefer to take "cash out," you can refinance your mortgage and borrow against your equity. Remember, though, that the $10,000 you take out of your mortgage is rolled into your monthly payment at the same interest

rate as your loan, so if you're paying 6 percent for your mortgage, your $10,000 would need to earn at least that much to break even.

Once all debts other than your home mortgage are paid, start putting the money that was going toward debt reduction into a new bank account paying the highest interest with minimal risk for a specific duration of time. The goal here is to build your own capital start-up fund for the new business as fast as possible. (The things you'll spend it on will be detailed in Chapter 7.)

When this financial plan is complete, you will be able to estimate the time it will take to accomplish each goal, barring any financial disasters such as job loss or divorce. Then you can wisely invest your monthly savings payment in a plan that is based on your time frame. Talk to a financial planner for help to find the right risk-to-reward ratio to safely grow your capital fund on your schedule.

My recommendation is that you play it safe and take a low-risk money market or certificate of deposit (CD) interest rate rather than investing in a short-term stock market fund. The Dow/Nasdaq have been basically flat over the past several years (as of mid-2005). Grow your savings safely (investment-wise) but fast (deposit-rate-wise) by putting as much cash into your business start-up fund as you can. After you accumulate $10K to $15K, set up a second separate bank account for home expenses and budget needs.

This second fund will be much larger than the one required for starting your consulting business. Exactly how much you'll need will depend on your lifestyle and consumption, along with the amount of remaining debt you will have after you've moved.

Another factor to consider is whether or not your spouse is working now or will be working after the move. If your family is currently dependent on both incomes just to pay the bills, accumulating enough to make your move possible will be a long and difficult task. However, if you are living well within your means, things will proceed more smoothly and quickly.

Realistically, your new consulting business will take a year to pull in $25K, two years for $50K, and maybe four to five years for more than $100K. Some of you will do better sooner, and others will struggle at first. During those initial very lean months of income as a rural computer consultant, you will definitely be living mostly off that second account set up to pay for the basics of life. The size of that account will determine how much time you've got to start picking up clients, bringing in a reliable amount of consulting income, and being able to meet your optimized financial obligations.

To come up with a goal amount for the second account to cover your post-move household needs, set up an Excel spreadsheet and forecast a monthly budget including all fixed and variable costs of living. Make sure you work in the inflation rate for most consumables and a higher rate for taxes and insurance.

During the first couple of years of our own limited-income period, we saw our health insurance premiums nearly double from $450 a month to $800, and our homeowners' insurance jump from $1,500 up to $2,000 a year. Health insurance is another pesky challenge to overcome in your financial preparation. Like many other American families, our family has members with a so-called existing condition, which significantly complicates getting health insurance.

Pre-existing conditions pretty much end any possibility of acquiring private health insurance, which is much more affordable than group health insurance. The "existing condition" locked us into establishing a group health-care plan under the consulting business. However you accomplish it, having health-care insurance for your family is critical and mandatory, and you must factor it into your financial plan and include it in the goal amount for your home expenses account.

You will grow to appreciate how much your current employer is paying for your family's health-care insurance when you find out how much it will be for you to fund the whole monthly amount by yourself on an after-tax basis. You have probably heard about COBRA — a plan to extend your current employer's group health-care insurance plan up to 18 months after you leave that company. The problem is that you pay both portions rather than just your couple of hundred a month (as is deducted from your paycheck today). Don't be surprised if the total COBRA extended health-care plan runs $1,000 or more per month.

Canada has a universal health-care system that provides primary medical care to all Canadian citizens and permanent residents. Health care comes under the jurisdiction of provincial/territorial governments, and only three provinces — Alberta, British Columbia, and Ontario — charge a health premium. In other provinces and territories, basic health care is paid for through tax revenue. In the provinces that charge medical premiums, the fees vary based on family income. In British Columbia, for example, a family of four with an income of $60,000 would pay monthly premiums of $108; in Alberta the rates are slightly lower.

In addition to the universal coverage, many people who are employed have access to group plans for extended medical benefits. Employers often pay one-half or more of such premiums, so when you make the transition to being self-employed in Canada, you must also budget for increased health-insurance costs. Self-employed Canadians can get extended medical coverage (e.g., for prescription drugs, dental care, vision care, physiotherapy) through companies such as Blue Cross and Manulife Financial. Depending on the extent of coverage, the premiums for a family of four can total several hundred dollars per month — considerably less than for comparable coverage in the US.

Post-move financial tasks

Before you make your move, be sure you understand that you'll need to stay as frugal after your move as you were in preparation for it. To remain financially solvent during the first couple of years, and to avoid quickly depleting the household expense fund that was supposed to last three years, you will need to halt impulse purchases. Try to put off that expensive trip to the Caymans for another couple of years and wait for the price of that awesome plasma TV to come down significantly.

You will have to watch your gasoline consumption, too, if you live ten or more minutes away from the small town where you buy your groceries, take the kids to school, and visit your clients. Make sure your trips are multipurpose and try to avoid duplicating any trips with your spouse, since the increased driving distances can quickly drive your gas bill to $500 a month or more.

One of the major benefits of rural living and small towns are the lower costs of things such as private schools. Since the per capita incomes in small rural towns are much lower than in big cities, the cost of private schooling is dramatically lower, too. Our grade-school-aged girls are attending, for a combined cost of less than $500 a month, a wonderful church-based private school that is accredited by the state of Texas. In Houston, that cost would easily top $700 per child per month!

Many states and provinces have an agricultural-property tax exemption if you raise livestock or grow crops (such as hay) on your land. This tax exemption, found only in rural areas, has benefited us greatly by cutting our property taxes by almost 70 percent. The property taxes on our ranch, if it were in Houston, would be more than $1,000 a month ($12K a year), whereas here in the country, I pay about $3,500 a year.

Many other activities, for example martial arts classes and Kindermusik activities for the kids, are roughly half the cost of their sister companies in the big cities.

Plan to turn that budget-forecasting spreadsheet you'll have created during your pre-move financial planning into a rolling monthly budget and spending log. You can do this by accounting for everything you spend on a monthly basis by listing all expenses as line items. Each Excel row (or line item) will have a column for what the expense was for, how much it was, when it was spent, and whether it was paid for by debit (not credit) card, check, or cash. At the end of the calendar month, you'll have a perfect log of exactly how much you spent and what you spent it on, which will enable you to better budget for the next month. In Excel, you can just copy that worksheet to the next sheet and rename it with the next month's name.

Financial software for the home — such as Microsoft Money and Intuit's Quicken — can also perform this function, but with less manual upkeep. However you do it, use some sort of strict accounting to make sure you stick with your monthly home budget.

Once you have killed the debt monkey by eliminating as much debt as possible before you move, make darn sure you don't resurrect the monkey to haunt you again and put all you've accomplished in jeopardy. Being out of debt is one of the best feelings to experience and will help you sleep at night.

Though money may get tight during your first few years as a rural computer consultant, stick with your original plan: be frugal in your household spending and avoid new debt in all forms like the plague.

This goes for your consulting business as well. Try very hard to avoid business loans, business credit cards, and even lines of credit. Operate your company on a cash basis. Pay yourself after you have paid all the payroll taxes, and only if you still have money in the bank for hardware and software purchases to make money on material sales to your clients. Keep a good buffer of at least $1,000 in the business checking account and monitor all transactions closely on a daily basis.

Consider all of these factors and recommendations when compiling your plan and beginning the preparation for your big change of life as a rural computer consultant.

Choosing a Small Town

Choosing the right small town to start your new life as a rural computer consultant will be one of the most important and challenging decisions you'll ever make. It is already common knowledge that some of the highest stress events of one's life are changing jobs and moving to a new home. This project requires you to do both at the same time. Though your overall goal is to reduce the stress in your work and home environment by simplifying your workplace and migrating to a peaceful homestead, getting there can be an interesting journey.

It took us more than a year to find the right homestead to buy, back in 1997. At that time, I had no idea I was going to be doing the type of small-town consulting I am successfully performing now. After looking at places an hour or more west of Austin out in the desert and rock, we found land that was cheap but too isolated from our friends and family. Having them make an hour or two-hour drive to come visit us was one thing, but asking them to trek four or more hours one way was pushing it.

We looked at flatland, wooded areas, hills with views, and deep hidden locations. For months, we visited small farmhouses with big acreages and big ranch homes on less than ten acres. Once, we looked at a property for sale that had more than 400 acres on the side of a west Texas mountain, without any home or buildings, for less than $500 per acre.

Finally, our realtor took us up to a remodeled farmhouse built in 1881 on a slight rolling hill with 115 acres, just eight miles west of Brenham, Texas. Since Brenham was just an hour's drive northwest of Houston, the distance was right. In fact, our soon-to-be ranch home was directly in the middle of the drive between Houston and Austin, where we also had family and friends. The sellers were in their late 70s and were anxious to sell the home they had fixed up so nicely. Since this was back in 1997, it was before the massive real estate rush sent property values skyrocketing.

We lucked out finding this home and were very fortunate that it was located near the prosperous, growing, quaint, conservative, and yet still small town of Brenham. Since I was trying to get out of the computer business when we bought our place, we did no research on business opportunities. Nor did we look into the quality of the local schools, since my wife and I did not plan to have children at that time and my son, Dustin, was still living with his mother.

Things just fell into place when I decided to start Deans Consulting and try my hand at small-town consulting. All the right factors were already in place due to our great and lucky choice of our new home and its location near a wonderful small town.

Now that I know all those factors and their relevance to small-town computer consulting, we need to go through them so you can make the right choice based on known requirements and specific issues. I want you to be able to choose your location based on research and knowledge of the realities of living and working in a rural small town. In other words, I don't want you to rely on making a lucky choice like I made when we bought our country place.

Choosing a rural home is a very important decision. And as I've already discussed, you also have to have other bases covered, such as support from your spouse and all the necessary financial planning.

Now let's get down to the nuts and bolts of choosing the right small town for you and your family. If you are happy with the state or province you're living in now, then start right there and look at all towns in all directions that are a one- to three-hour drive away. The rural life can be found in under a two-hour drive from almost any major city.

One reason that it's a good idea to start looking locally within a 200-mile radius is that it's likely you'll have ties to where you are located now. Those ties may be your and your spouse's families, close friends, or business associates and contacts. It will be less of a traumatic change moving an hour or two away rather than somewhere that requires a half day's drive or, worse yet, a plane ride.

If you are a divorced parent and your child spends time with both you and your former spouse, you cannot choose a small town that's far away from your child's other parent. I have very strong opinions on this subject, since my former wife moved my son from Houston to Dallas and then from Dallas to Alaska. You cannot make this move without first considering how that distance will affect your children.

If you have stepchildren under your roof, you must not move them away from your spouse's former wife or husband if that parent is currently close enough to enjoy weekly visitations. This goes double for you parents whose kids live with an ex-spouse but get to see you on a regular but intermittent basis. You cannot and must not move so far away that the already diminished time spent with your kids is lessened even further. If the small town is less than a two-hour drive away from where your child lives, it *can* work if both parties are cooperating.

However, if you don't have children, and you have few roots in your current location and see little opportunity in the area (due to no growth or even recession), it may be time to look farther afield to areas that are growing and expanding. Watch the *Wall Street Journal* for articles showing high-growth cities and then look for small rural towns within 100 miles of them. When big cities make money and expand their businesses, their satellite small towns also benefit and grow. Stay away from areas that are dependent on depressed major markets since that will have a negative effect on surrounding rural areas.

Look for a town that mirrors your beliefs, culture, and political makeup. To start up a business in a small town, it is a good idea for you to be among your own kind of people. That may seem biased or small minded, but remember that you are starting a business, and people prefer to do business with others like themselves, because it makes them feel comfortable.

Surf the Internet thoroughly and come up with a list of small towns with populations between 10,000 and 50,000 that are surrounded by farms and ranches. Explore the county- and town-sponsored websites and analyze all information related to the health of the business environments, demographics, education resources, and taxes.

One great source of information about a town's business health is that town's chamber of commerce. You can find the website for a town's chamber of commerce by doing a Google search specifying the town or county name along with "chamber of commerce." View the membership roster and do a rough

count of businesses — keeping in mind that not all businesses will be listed, but the majority of them will. Next, call the chamber of commerce during the week and ask them if their membership is growing, stable, or declining. Ask for specific membership numbers over the past three to five years. This will tell you the real story about that community's economic health.

Next you will want to contact that county's appraisal district (or municipality's property assessment office) and look up property-tax rates, appraised-value increases, and the area's overall financial picture.

A good rule of thumb to determine if a town is too small to start your rural computer consulting business is to make sure it has a McDonald's and a Wal-Mart. If the town does not have both, drive on through. Also, look for a small town that is in a cluster of small towns, all within a half hour's drive from the center where you will be living. I have active clients located in a half a dozen small towns within a 30-minute drive of my home base of Brenham.

After you have found an economically healthy small town, it will be time for a weekend visit to check things out more closely. Locate a local phone book to check out the number of businesses listed, along with the types of products and services they offer. Also, search for any computer-repair stores, consultants, or technicians listed in the Yellow Pages for that area.

While you are driving around the township, watch carefully for new construction areas and a low number of For Rent signs on storefronts. Occupied, active, and thriving retail areas along with new commercial projects being built are prime signs of strong economic health for small towns.

During this discovery period, check out the schools, churches, parks, and stores to make sure the basic needs of your family will be met. If your spouse is a devout Catholic like mine is, you will want to verify the existence of a flourishing parish at a nearby Catholic church.

The town of Burton (pop. 311) has a single senior high school, in which the senior class is usually less than 20 students, so we decided to send my son Dustin, who came to live with us shortly after we moved here, to nearby Brenham High School instead. With graduating classes topping 500, this school offered more choice of extracurricular activities such as the Marine Corp Junior ROTC, which Dustin was in for all four years.

Once you have found a charming small town that is economically sound and is surrounded by a peaceful countryside with affordable rural homes, it is time to find a good deal on your future homestead. Utilize the Internet and find a realtor from that area who knows the people who are selling, what they are selling, and why they are selling it, along with most of the history that goes with the property. Remember our discussion about financial planning, and look for and purchase a home that will suit your long-term needs within a wise and tightly managed budget.

One critical issue concerning finding and choosing your new country home is the availability of high-speed broadband Internet access. Specifically, you'll need at least 512Mb/s downstream and 256Mb/s upstream bandwidth to the Internet from your prospective new home. When we first bought our ranch, we were limited to only dial-up Internet service providers (ISPs). When I started up Deans Consulting a year later, the dial-up limitation was killing my productivity. Our only higher-speed choice was satellite Internet access via StarBand, which cost $800 start-up and $75 a month. After a few years of StarBand, a land-based wireless company called Texas Broadband began delivering Internet access to our county, and I immediately made a business contact with them.

Since there are distance limitations with both DSL and cable ISPs, you will need to research your high-speed Internet options *before* you purchase a house in the country to make sure you are not limiting yourself on Internet bandwidth.

In other words, do not buy a home down in a valley with trees all around cutting off a good line of sight, which can knock out the chance of wireless Internet service. Satellite Internet service will not suit your needs due to limited upstream bandwidth and vulnerability to weather.

The same goes for cellular service. Make sure your cell phone works well from inside the home you are looking at before making an offer on it. Since you will be getting business calls from clients on your cell while you're at the house, make sure the cellular signal is at least two bars for reliable voice communications.

You need to keep a lot in mind when you're trying to find the right small town to start your new life and venture. To help simplify the process and make it easier for you to evaluate each small town you consider, I've developed the Small-Town Assessment. Have a look at Checklist 1.

CHECKLIST 1
SMALL-TOWN ASSESSMENT

	Yes	No
Are there any computer-repair stores, consultants, or technicians in the area?		
Are there any extracurricular activities for children?		
Are there any new commercial projects being built?		
Are there any parks nearby?		
Are there churches available?		
Are there good schools available?		
Are there other towns clustered around it?		
Are there stores where basic items can be purchased?		
Does it have a chamber of commerce?		
Does it have a McDonald's?		
Does it have a Wal-Mart?		
Is a high-speed, broadband Internet connection available?		
Is the retail area occupied, active, and thriving?		
Does it have a branch of a well-known bank?		
Does it have a low crime rate?		
Are the property values increasing rather than decreasing?		
Does the town have its own newspaper?		
Does the town have its own hospital and/or health clinic?		
Does your current insurance cover the services at the town's health-care facilities?		
Are these the type of people (in terms of culture, politics, background, etc.) that you could be comfortable doing business with?		

7

Your Business Plan and Pre-Move Marketing Research

It's crucial that you carefully sort out all the family and financial aspects of your move before you go ahead with it. But there's more for you to do. To make certain your new business will succeed, at the same time as you're building up your start-up fund and looking at small towns, you also need to create a business plan for yourself and conduct marketing research.

Business Plan

In the previous chapter, I mentioned an account that you need to set up, a fund to provide your own private investment capital. This account will finance your new consulting business for the first six months and should provide the majority of the business tools I found necessary to perform computer-consulting services for small companies in rural towns. But even before you start creating your spending list for your new consulting company, you will need to have a clear-cut written plan.

Before you can get any moneymaking project off the ground, you must develop and document a business plan. There are numerous books and websites that can help you write a business plan. I highly recommend using such resources. Since I actually fell into what I call rural computer consulting, I never developed such a business plan, and I ended up wasting thousands of dollars on misdirected subprojects and ventures that did not make me any money.

A business plan will help you address all concerns and lay out a specific road map for your new operation. A good source for developing your business plan is Small Business Administration (www.SBA.gov), which offers a decent template you can use free of charge. (Canadian readers can contact their local branch of the Canada Business Network, www.cbsc.org.) Most business plan templates, including the SBA's, contain the following sections:

- Executive summary
- Market analysis
- Company description
- Organization and management
- Marketing and sales management
- Service or product line
- Funding request
- Financials
- Appendix

Though some parts of the SBA's generic plan won't apply to you (for example, the parts that address management structures and multiple employee issues), most of it will be quite helpful for you to think about and use to write your own explicit business plan.

The market analysis portion of the plan is basically the results of your research of the area you are looking to move to and the computer services that local businesses require. The company description will explain how you as the primary consultant will be providing computer services along with hardware and software sales to your small-town clients.

The organization and management section of your business plan will describe how the primary employee — you — will wear many hats in the company. These roles will include sales, marketing, accounting, collecting, and of course consulting, as well as every other little task that comes along with running your new company.

Chapters 4 and 5 of this book described 40 services and the skill sets required to provide those services in small towns. Pick the top 10 or 20 services you know you can immediately provide, and that will be the

meat of the service or product line section of the plan.

Since you'll have set up an account to provide the start-up capital, a simple statement that you will be 100 percent privately funded as the owner will address both the funding request and financials parts of the business plan.

It is well known that the top three reasons for small businesses to fail are the following:

1. Lack of experience
2. Insufficient capital (money)
3. Poor location

As long as you can provide 10 of the most requested computer-related services discussed in Chapter 4, you can avoid the first reason for small-business failure. Chapter 6 addressed the issue of your choice of small town, which is critical to your success as a rural computer consultant; so, as long as you do your homework, you can eliminate the third cause of small-business failure. The second reason (insufficient capital) is what we really need to focus on now.

During the first two years of Deans Consulting, I spent lots of money on things I thought I needed based on the work I had done back in the big city. To save you that expense, I have created a start-up cost chart that shows a list of recommended hardware, software, service, and other business expenses you will need to fund during the first six months to one year of your operation. Sample 2 shows all items sorted by highest cost and then sorted by order of importance.

You will not have to invest all this money during the first month, but I highly recommend that you save up a minimum of $12,000

START-UP COSTS

Start-up Costs — Sorted by Cost of Items

Item Description	Cost ($)
PC Workstation with MS Office	1,500
General liability insurance (first year)	1,500
Mobile troubleshooting laptop	1,200
Client hardware/software purchases	1,000
Initial marketing	1,000
WhatsUp Professional or SolarWinds network-monitoring software	1,000
MS FrontPage, MS Project, Adobe Photoshop, SWiSH	700
Books on Windows support	500
Setup of corporation or LLC	500
Palm PDA/Smartphone with accessories	400
Company dress shirts (10) with your logo	350
Miscellaneous start-up expenses	300
QuickBooks financial software	250
QuickBooks setup and training from CPA (CA in Canada)	250
Chamber of commerce membership	200
Color printer, scanner, fax combo	200
Basic office supplies	200
QuickBooks payroll subscription	200
Six months of website and other online services	200
UTP cable tester, RJ45 crimper, and UTP CAT5E cable	200
CD-ROM business card setup	100
1GB USB Flash/Thumb drive	100
Double-window envelopes for invoices	100
Business cards (500 paper)	50
Total Recommended Start-up Capital	**$12,000**

Start-up Costs — Sorted by Highest Priority Item

Item Description	Cost ($)
Business cards (500 paper)	50
PC Workstation with MS Office	1,500
General liability insurance (first year)	1,500
Setup of corporation or LLC	500
UTP cable tester, RJ45 crimper, and UTP CAT5E cable	200
1GB USB Flash/Thumb drive	100
Palm PDA/Smartphone with accessories	400
Company dress shirts (10) with your logo	350
QuickBooks financial software	250
QuickBooks setup and training from CPA (CA in Canada)	250
QuickBooks payroll subscription	200
Color printer, scanner, fax combo	200
Chamber of commerce membership	200
Client hardware/software purchases	1,000
Basic office supplies	200
Six months of website and other online services	200
Initial marketing	1,000
Books on Windows support	500
WhatsUp Professional or SolarWinds network-monitoring software	1,000
MS FrontPage, MS Project, Adobe Photoshop, SWiSH	700
Mobile troubleshooting laptop	1,200
CD-ROM business card setup	100
Double-window envelopes for invoices	100
Miscellaneous start-up expenses	300
Total Recommended Start-up Capital	**$12,000**

for initial capital investment and for your first six months of expenses. The more you build up the business start-up account before you move to a small town, the better your company's cash flow will be.

As the initial few months go by, you may have to slow down your capital spending, depending on your first business activities and cash flow. You want to avoid spending all your start-up capital during the first couple of weeks, so you don't end up short on cash, waiting for more business to develop.

When projects and troubleshooting sessions do start paying off and the monthly invoices start producing monthly checks in the mail, you can start to use that income as additional start-up funding. You can also leave some of your original cash as a buffer for slower business times and for rainy days.

Take your time developing your plan and crunching the start-up cost numbers in a spreadsheet as in Sample 2 (a blank copy of this form can be found on the CD-ROM that accompanies this book). Read as many books and articles as you can get your hands on about starting businesses and writing business plans. After you have a good draft of your plan, show it to one or two business peers whom you can trust, and start discussing your idea. You may get some jeers and discouraging comments, but keep your attitude positive while taking in constructive comments and concerns.

One thing I learned years ago was to not take advice on ventures from people who had failed in their own pursuit of those same ventures. Instead, to truly come up with a winning game plan, seek out counsel from those who've succeeded in the endeavor you are interested in. In other words, walk with the wise and not with the naysayers.

Pre-Move Marketing Research

After you have found the perfect small town with a growing economy and chosen a nice home, you will have a few weeks (if not a couple of months) before the big move to perform some research on your future rural client base. Since most people will have to sell their current house to purchase their next home, the move from big-city life to small-town living will be a clean "cutover."

However, some of you may want to try out rural living on weekends to get a feel of it, even after purchasing a home in a rural area. If finances allow this and you are able to handle two mortgages (along with the tax and insurance payments), the weekend mode may settle any big-move jitters or concerns you have about making such a large change in your family's life. This is, of course, if you purchase a rural home close enough to your city home to make weekend trips feasible. It took us a year of weekends and workweek holidays visiting our country home and learning about our small rural town for my wife to get used to the whole idea.

So whether you are waiting for your city house to sell or are doing weekend visits, there is work to be done preparing to make contact with your future small-town clients. As mentioned in the previous chapter, the town or county chamber of commerce is a great place to start. Physically visit it, talk to the people working there, and join the organization. You'll need to have already chosen some kind of company name and have decided if your company will be a single-owner corporation or a limited liability company (LLC). To join, you'll have to give a phone number, so use your cell phone number rather than your city home phone.

The fees to join most small-town chamber of commerce organizations are usually around $100 per year, and you'll find it's well worth it. One of the big benefits of joining is that you can get the directory of membership for that area. This will be in booklet format; however, if you request it, they may provide you with a disk of the membership data in a spreadsheet or raw-data format. If they give you only the hard copy of the membership directory, you can scan and OCR the document into your computer. If you don't have optical character recognition software, you or perhaps someone else in the family can type all the names, numbers, and addresses into an Excel spreadsheet.

It took my wife a couple of weeks to type the 500 companies listed in the Washington County membership directory into Excel, but it was a gold mine of accurate and up-to-date information on the majority of the businesses in our area. The great thing about this list is that it'll give you a good contact name of at least a manager of each business, if not the owner himself, along with the phone number and maybe even an e-mail address.

However you acquire the digital version of the chamber's membership directory, use it to create your first cold-call list. Though you can't start making cold sales calls yet, you can prepare the list in Excel by prioritizing it by company size and type of business. For example, you'll put the gas stations and gift shops at the bottom of the list and have the larger companies with office workers toward the top, since those companies have a greater need for computer support services. You may want to avoid the largest companies with hundreds of employees at first, since they will most likely have an in-house computer support person or already have an outside firm taking care of their IT needs.

The best group of small rural companies that I found were in the 5-to-50 employees range, and all lacked consistent computer support. Once I got my name out to them, many of them called me back to see if I could fix a computer problem they currently had. This initial sale sometimes happened right away, but most often occurred weeks if not months after my first cold call to them.

So the goal here is to prepare a great cold-call lead list in an Excel spreadsheet to be ready to hit the ground running as a rural computer consultant. We will talk more about the initial marketing effort in Chapters 11 and 13, and this spreadsheet will be a focal point in our discussion.

With the chamber membership list and the local Yellow Pages in hand, drive around during the workweek in your new town to see where the activity is hot. Look for numerous cars parked in employee parking spaces and notice activity at the loading areas where delivery trucks arrive. Look at the landscaping and see how well kept the company's grounds are, since this will give you a hint of their financial health.

Back in 1999 when I realized that I wanted to return to the computer industry, I started noticing how many computers were in the companies I was already doing consumer business with (e.g., auto dealerships, insurance companies, and hardware stores). There was opportunity everywhere I looked in our small town. Someone had to manage the hardware and software issues and upgrades, so it might as well be me.

During your daily routine of visiting local businesses, also check out their version of Windows and the age of their computers. Casually ask how their computers are working and what kind of Internet access they have. Notice if anyone is waiting on their PC to respond, or is frustrated with the computer software during your shopping visits. Make notes in your prospect spreadsheet about these observations to better prepare yourself for the upcoming round of cold calls.

Next, you need to find out who your competition is in your new small town. Odds are there is only one computer person, or maybe two, but you will need to visit and talk with them. There could also be an established computer store that builds and sells PCs. Depending on your first impression of them, you can mention that you're thinking about starting a consulting business in the area. The computer store people may see you as a threat, but they may also see you as a new customer who will be buying a potentially large amount of hardware and software from them. Try to put them at ease, and help them understand that you'll be performing a one-on-one specialized service with more hand-holding than they offer.

Ask them how busy they are and notice the fixed and to-be-fixed computers at the pick-up and drop-off areas. During your discovery routine, swing by a few times and observe the number of cars in front of their store. Also, note the number of technicians they have in the back of the shop and what the store's hours are.

If you can, find out how much of their time is spent working on computers at the store compared to time spent at clients' offices. On-site support is the main area of overlap and competition you will have with them, but sooner or later you'll have to work with the local computer guys.

Along with preparing your prospect list, learning about the local business community, and scoping out the competition, you'll need to get ready to pull the trigger on your new career as a rural computer consultant. For that, you'll need to have at least a company name "DBA" (doing business as) filed with the county or provincial tax office. Get some business cards made with your cell phone number as the primary work number, along with a reliable e-mail address. Be sure to use your new postal address on your business cards rather than using a P.O. box.

Now all that's left is for the right buyer to come along and close on your city house. This will enable you to escape from the urban rat race and begin your new consulting adventure in the peaceful country. Once the old house is sold, you can make a beeline to your new small-town home and start a new life.

PART 4

START-UP

8

Settling In and Starting Your Business

The weeks following your move to the country will be the busiest of your life. You and your family will be settling in to your new, small-town life, and you'll be starting your new business. This chapter details the first steps you'll need to take to get your rural computer consulting business off to a solid start.

After the Move

For those few of you who tried the weekend visits, fell in love with the rural area, and are now ready to the join the majority who did the cutover by immediately selling the city house, it is time to settle in and make a go of this new life.

The transition to any new permanent residence can be challenging, but moving from the big city to the little town or from a noisy suburban house to a quiet country home can cause culture shock. The more populous the area you come from, the more of a contrast you'll see and feel. It took me more than a month to sleep well at night

without hearing noises from cars or helicopters like I was used to in Houston. All I could hear was the blood rushing in my head due to the absolute silence during the nighttime at our ranch.

You will also experience a whole new sense of friendliness from small-town people compared to city dwellers. Families in rural areas, though physically separated by acres and sometimes miles of empty gravel roads, learn to rely on each other and become much closer than the neighbors who live less than 30 feet apart and who briefly wave to each other in the city. In most cases, the closer people physically live next to each other, the less they know about each other.

Within three years of our move to the country, we knew every family and homestead within a one-mile radius of our ranch. Many of them dropped by during the first month or so just to introduce themselves. We soon got the idea and started visiting others who lived farther down the road. We watch each other's homes when one of us is away. We keep an eye out for loose livestock and fence problems, and we loan and borrow farming implements and tools. For several years, my wife and I threw a Fourth of July party for the dozen or so neighborhood families, and most of them attended on a regular basis.

The openness and maybe the dialect of your new town will be different from what you have been used to in the city, but over time, you'll grow to like this new environment. It was an immediate delight for me, but it took a couple of years for my wife to get into the country groove. That's why I made such a point of the family move issues I discussed earlier in the book. It's important that you have your spouse's commitment to help you make this endeavor work for the family.

Before you start hitting the small-town streets and cold-calling to drum up business, you will need to get your home base set up and your family settled down. This may take a few weeks, but it is better to have your spouse happy and comfortable in your family's new setting before you jump into your new business. And even if you're single, there are still some issues that need to be addressed before you get started.

First, get moved in completely. Make sure all household appliances and fixtures are working properly, as the home inspector said they did when you closed on the new home. The big items are the water well and septic system. Without these two major items functioning properly, you cannot move forward.

As a test, you may want to flush all the toilets multiple times over a 30-minute period and make sure the sewage does not back up or the commodes cease to flush entirely. This will push a good load on the water well, which will give you the opportunity to listen to the pump and the tank's delivery system to verify that it is working properly. A good time to do this test of the septic system is when the ground is already wet from a recent rain. Also, since most well water contains calcium — which is what we call hard water — test out the water-softening equipment to make sure that it is operating properly.

Next, get a shotgun, go out at night an hour after sunset, and look for varmints like possums, armadillos, and skunks to start the elimination process. I had to wipe out a dozen of those stinky rabies-laden pests the first year, and more than twenty of them in the years following. Make sure the kids know about the risks, including snakes, spiders, and poison ivy, and the dangers of farm equipment. If your new rural home is off a gravel road, you will want to get an air compressor and a tire-repair kit because you will get numerous flat tires, which usually show up in the morning.

After your landline phone service and satellite-dish TV are set up and functioning, the next thing is to get your high-speed Internet access established and operational. Remember, satellite Internet access will not cut it, so you'd better have chosen a place with wireless Internet coverage, as was recommended in Chapter 6. If you are close enough to town and are within range of DSL or cable Internet access, then make sure you purchase a strong enough package to provide ample bandwidth both downstream and upstream.

Set up your new business address to match your new rural home address rather than using a P.O. box. This will help give you a rural identity, which will attract more clients than if you look like an out-of-town big-city guy trying to do business in a small town. Put your home address on your business cards and make sure your physical mailbox is labeled properly and in good shape, since all your checks will arrive in it.

Immediately start up a subscription to the local newspaper for home delivery. This is a great source of the local business scene and social activities. You will be amazed at what makes the printed news in a small town. If anyone gets a little award, he or she appears in the paper. If anyone gets into a wreck, his or her smashed car is pictured in the paper. If anyone gets in any trouble, he or she gets the front page of the local paper.

Compared to city newspapers, small-town papers also feature more positive stories, which is a refreshing change. There is often a more conservative tone to the local newspaper, mirroring the character of the majority of rural small towns, which usually lean to the right politically.

Carefully read the local paper, take note of the employment section, and watch for companies that are in a hiring mode. The more "help wanted" ads you see in the paper, the more likely it is that those companies are growing and will need your services.

If you get a donation request in the mail from the local volunteer fire department, send them $20 or so to support their vital work in the community. It's just good public relations. You want to cover the bases and not get off to a bad start in a new area. Another good reason to send a few dollars to this good cause is that it will score you points with the local volunteer firefighters, who may be among your future clients and may remember your name from the donation card.

Do your best to quickly blend in and start putting down roots in the new community. If you are a person of faith, start attending the local church of your choice and get to know the congregation members. The vast majority of my clients attend one church or another in Brenham, and the practice of religion is a common custom that is practically expected by all around my area. This is probably the case in your rural small town — and this may convince you to attend church on a regular basis.

Business Activation

Once you've settled into your new homestead and your family has started adjusting to their new environment, it's time for you to get cracking with your new business.

You will need to set aside a remote and quiet place in your rural home to serve as your home office. Pick a room that has Internet access, a good cell phone signal, and can be closed off from household noise, kids, and other distractions. (Chapter 9 will discuss the home office setup in more detail.)

To officially start your business as a rural computer consultant, you will need to accomplish the following tasks. These should be done before you start cold-calling your potential clients, and those of you with more initiative can even begin the process before leaving the big city:

1. Pick a company name for your new consulting business.

2. Register a matching or related domain name for your website.

3. Establish a "Doing Business As" (DBA) under that name.

4. Incorporate your business by setting up a single-owner corporation or LLC.

5. Contact the IRS to get an employer identification number (EIN). (Canadian readers will need to contact the Canada Revenue Agency (CRA) to get a business number (BN).)

6. Apply for a sales-tax registration if your state or province has a sales tax.

7. Migrate or rename existing capital account(s) to the new business name.

8. Purchase a general liability insurance policy for at least the first year.

Let's briefly cover these eight tasks so you can understand their importance and order of execution.

Company name

When picking a company name, keep it short and simple. I set mine up as Deans Consulting, LLC, for instant name and business-type recognition. Steer away from fancy-sounding, difficult-to-spell, or foreign-themed names. If your last name is Jones, try something like "Jones Computer Services, Inc." or "Jones Consulting." You may have to alter your company's name if there already is a DBA in the jurisdiction using that same name.

Domain name

You may have to align your choice of company name with the availability of at least a similar domain name for your company website. As I explained earlier, originally, my company website and domain name was LanWanDesign.com because DeansConsulting.com was already taken. I initially chose LanWanDesign.com because my existing skills were limited mainly to networking rather than SOHO and desktop support. Test the availability for your top choices at GoDaddy.com, and, since GoDaddy.com is so inexpensive, register the best one you can get for at least two years.

DBA application

After coming up with a simple company name and a related domain name, make a trip to the local courthouse and file for a DBA (Doing Business As) in person rather than by phone. You want to get out in the community, meet the townspeople, and start getting your name and face recognized. It usually costs less than $50 to get a DBA and requires only a simple single-page application.

In Canada, if you are incorporating your business, you will need to do a name search. In some provinces you can go online and do a search through the NUANS system and in others, you will need to complete a Name Reservation or Approval Request form through the local government registry.

Incorporation

Using your new company name, the next step is to set up a single-owner corporation to limit your personal liability, in case something goes terribly wrong. Depending on your state or province's incorporation laws, you will want to draft articles of incorporation. In the US, you have the option of creating either an S corporation (Inc.) or limited liability company (LLC). In Canada, you have the option of creating a sole proprietorship or incorporating your business.

Creating a legal entity like an S corporation or an LLC can shield you personally from lawsuits and creditors. Since we live in a lawsuit-happy society in the US, I strongly advise you to research this carefully and even have a professional help you set it up properly. Just in case you have a really bad day and accidentally drop a client's laptop or wipe out a server that has not been backed up for months, you will want to protect yourself from unreasonable and vengeful hotheads.

I registered Deans Consulting as an LLC with the help of BixFilings (www.business filings.com), which charges anywhere from $99 for their basic service up to $349 for the full-service package. After I brought my wife onboard Deans Consulting to help me with paperwork, accounting, and marketing, I converted our company to an S corporation by filling out a couple of forms from the IRS.

In Canada, a sole proprietorship is not an incorporated business, but it does have the advantage of low start-up costs when you are just beginning your business. The biggest disadvantage is that you have unlimited liability, which means you will personally assume all the risks and debts of your company. As a sole proprietor, you may be required to register with the local government registry under your business name.

The advantage of incorporating is that your company will have limited liability, which means you are protected personally from lawsuits and creditors. To incorporate provincially or territorially, you will need to register and license your company through the local government registrar's office. You can register and pay the fees by mail or online.

However you decide to incorporate, consult a professional in your state or province about incorporating and consult a CPA or CGA about your company's tax issues.

Employer identification number

To start writing yourself payroll checks, you will need to pay the IRS or CRA those dreaded payroll taxes. Before you can do this, you'll need to contact the IRS or CRA and acquire an employer identification number (EIN) (or, for Canadian readers, a business number (BN)), which is like a social security number for businesses. During the conversation you'll have with the IRS agent, you should also request that the quarterly 941 payroll forms be mailed to you on a regular basis. We will talk about business tax issues later in this book, but for right now, you'll need that EIN to do a few other administrative tasks. (Additionally, Canadian readers will need to contact the CRA to set up their company's CRA accounts.)

Sales tax registration

If your state or province has a sales tax like Texas does, you will need to contact the comptroller's office and talk to someone who knows about the computer industry. Around 2002, there was a change to the Texas taxation statutes that subjected computer services and some consulting services to state sales tax. Luckily I heard about it through the professional grapevine, but I was getting conflicting advice from my consulting peers. Half of them swore they did not have to collect and pay sales tax on their services and the other half swore they did.

I went straight to the source by calling the Texas comptroller's office in Austin, and was directed to the person in charge of those technical professions that fell under the new sales tax guidelines. He was able to explicitly list all the activities that were subjected to sales taxes after the change and the few that were not. From that point on, to avoid any tax problems with the state, I billed, collected, and paid sales taxes on the services I offered that were listed as taxable.

In addition to paying your payroll taxes, you must have a clear understanding of the sales tax laws in your state or province and comply fully. Do not ignore them and end up with a five-figure fine and levy against your company.

Company bank account

After all the company naming issues have been resolved, it's time to transfer that $12K you have saved up into a new bank account in your small rural town. Having a local corporate bank account is critical to enable you to quickly deposit the numerous checks per month you will one day be receiving in your mailbox.

Since the checks from your clients will be written to your company name rather than your personal name, you must set up this new bank account under the company name. Make sure that the bank offers a credit/debit card and electronic access over the Internet so you can closely monitor the transactions. You may also want to set up a second account at that same bank as a personal family checking account, to which you can deposit the paychecks written from your company's bank account. The combined balances of the business and personal accounts usually help you qualify for better rates and services.

Liability insurance

Since we are on the subject of limiting your liability, you really should have a general liability insurance policy tailored for your computer consulting company. A good place to start is at www.Techinsurance.com, which has an online application system and can send you a quote in two business days. A single-person computer company can get $1,000,000 in coverage for around $1,200 per year, depending on the area and specific services offered.

I recommend acquiring an insurance policy like this for at least the first year, just in case you have to deal with a victim looking for an accident and waiting to sue someone. How many years you maintain the insurance is up to you. Surely, the best path is to keep paying the annual premiums and maintain your coverage.

Accounting System Configuration

As a rural computer consultant, you'll be wearing many hats throughout the workweek. The most important of these jobs is keeping your small-town clients happy, but the next is bookkeeping. The big issue here is getting your accounting system configured correctly, right from the beginning.

During the first four years of operating Deans Consulting, I did all the company's accounting on a giant Excel spreadsheet. With a worksheet for every client every month, it quickly grew to an unmanageable size. I had other spreadsheets too, including my log of expenditures, my client and vendor database, a hardware and software inventory list, and a complicated, formula-rich workbook for payroll and taxes.

This system came to an abrupt end in 2004, when my business grew so fast that I was sending out as many as 40 invoices a month. The spreadsheet had become too confusing and time-consuming, and it was clearly time for my homegrown solution to evolve.

Finally, I bit the bullet and bought Intuit's QuickBooks 2004 Pro financial software for $250 to manage my company's accounting. The important lesson that I learned here was to hire a QuickBooks consultant who was also a CPA (certified public accountant).

I got the consultant's name from the website www.Intuit.com (for Canadian readers, go to www.Intuit.ca) under the Pro-Advisors button on their support page. For $300, this experienced and well-qualified consultant remotely accessed my workstation while I watched him set up my company in QuickBooks 2004 Pro. He analyzed my existing Excel spreadsheets and configured the initial structure for my customers, vendors, bank accounts, invoices, payroll, and time sheets. While he remotely accessed my QuickBooks PC from Houston, we were also talking on the phone and having an interactive training session on entering time sheets, customers, and vendor information. He was able to monitor my session and show me shortcuts and offer suggestions on how best to run my company with QuickBooks.

After two one-hour sessions, I was comfortable enough to start using QuickBooks, and started importing the previous month's data into my company database. A couple of weeks after that, we had a third session in which he demonstrated how to set up and run payroll from QuickBooks and generate corporate paychecks. After a few months of using QuickBooks, I was amazed that I had ever got along without it. I was particularly impressed with the reports that could easily be generated, such as my IRS Form 941 quarterly filings.

Don't waste the years I did toiling with Excel spreadsheets, which are only as good as your formulas and cell selections. After fully converting over to QuickBooks in 2004, I found several errors I had made in the invoices to my clients while using Excel. One such mistake was delivering and installing a $300 version of MS Office for a client who was never billed for it. QuickBooks flagged that error, which I had made months ago, using my old Excel procedure.

I strongly recommend getting your business started out on the right foot by purchasing the latest version of Intuit's QuickBooks and contracting one of their independent ProAdvisor consultants to help you set up your company file. With the use of high-speed broadband Internet access and remote access tools like Remote Desktop (built into Windows XP) or GoToMyPC.com, you can learn quickly and conveniently, without having to travel or take a formal class.

Even if you just have one or two clients, your QuickBooks consultant can show you how to enter them into the customers list. From there, you will learn how to enter the services you performed that week in the time sheet, and create checks for the hardware or software you purchased for that client. Next, it all comes together when you create an invoice and pick up the billable time, items, and expense entities associated with that client and time frame. When it comes time to pay yourself, you simply click on "Pay Employees," enter the gross pay amount, and QuickBooks calculates the payroll and income taxes. Just like that, your net pay is printed out on a customized company paycheck (available for purchase from Intuit). At the end of the quarter or month, you just click on "Pay Payroll Liabilities," and QuickBooks creates a check to the IRS to cover your Social Security, Medicare, Medicaid, and income taxes.

The payroll system in QuickBooks alone is worth its weight in gold. You do not want to get on the wrong side of the tax department, since they love to audit single-owner businesses and eat them for lunch if their financial books are not in order. I have a friend who didn't think he needed to withhold and pay the payroll taxes back in the late 1980s when he was doing contract programming. The IRS hit him with a $30,000 bill for back taxes, fines, and penalties. He is still trying to pay that off, and now his tax burden has just risen to more than twice that amount due to their unforgiving interest structure.

Same thing goes for the sales taxes if you have a sales tax in your state or province. QuickBooks can calculate, invoice, track, and pay all required sales tax to the proper state agency. Just before the sales tax is due, you click on "Pay Sales Tax," and QuickBooks creates a check to send out to pay the piper.

Bottom line: Pay your taxes, all your taxes, correctly and on time. Period.

As the months and years roll on, your QuickBooks company file (which is the primary database with all the information in it)

will grow. From the start, make sure you back up this critical file with a QBW filename extension on a daily basis to multiple locations. I have a Windows backup script that runs every night at midnight that copies my QuickBooks company file to another PC's hard drive. With my online backup solution provided by DataDepositBox.com, a second copy of my precious accounting database is uploaded to the off-site and secure online backup via the Internet. At the end of the year, I make a final copy of it to a CD-ROM, label it, and place it in my safe. If you have ever backed up files in your life, this is the most important file to back up.

To keep an eye on my bank account with its 500 or so transactions per year, I use Microsoft Money, since it interacts well with my small-town bank branch. The transaction list from MS Money provides me with a second ledger that I can cross-reference with my QuickBooks account to verify nothing got overlooked, overcharged, or lost. Eventually, I will also integrate that process into QuickBooks.

Setting up on QuickBooks costs $500 to $600, and you may be tempted to bypass it and just get by with an Excel spreadsheet, since you will only have a couple of clients at first. Take my advice: use your spare time and capital funding and set up your business accounting properly, right from the beginning. It will be a lot simpler for you to learn QuickBooks with only a couple of clients and vendors during your first month than it was for me, since I had to import 50 clients, 100 vendors, and six months of time sheet activity.

Website Setup

Once you have completed all the company start-up paperwork and administrative tasks, you need to set up your new company's website. Your corporate website will be an online brochure that will inform your prospective clients about your services, your experience and industry background, and your contact information. You can also use it to display any sample studies or published works you have produced.

Do not attempt to set up your own web server, since this would be too costly, time-consuming, and unreliable due to power issues and rural ISP downtime problems. There are numerous web-hosting services that can provide robust and reliable website and e-mail hosting for a fraction of what it would cost you. The other advantage is that the hosting service will also supply technical support either over the phone, by e-mail, or by chat.

As I mentioned earlier, the Webolocity hosting service I use provides me with a reseller account delivering 2GB of storage and 3GB of bandwidth for $25 per month. This not only provides Deans Consulting with a web presence, but also hosting for 20 other websites belonging to my clients, who pay me $15 a month for hosting services via subaccounts. Webolocity's cPanel management is a comprehensive interface that is easy to use and responds quickly. It provides an all-in-one vehicle to manage storage and bandwidth quotas and e-mail accounts, control spam, and configure website security.

Start out with a 1GB Webolocity reseller account for $15 a month and start using it by putting your company's website there. You can do this quickly by changing the DNS server entry on the service that administers your domain name, such as GoDaddy.com, Register.com, or NetworkSolutions.com. After the DNS change has been made and the two- or three-day period has elapsed for completion of the name-change propagation, you can start creating the company's website content and publishing it.

Even if you just have a single-page website for your company that lists your services, summarizes your qualifications, and displays all contact information, that's better than no web presence at all. The lack of a website for any computer-related business means instant death in the marketplace.

Preferably, your website will have multiple web pages, including the following: Introduction, About Us, Contact Information, and Services.

The "Introduction" page should display your company logo and include a mission statement describing your goal of delivering enterprise-level computer consulting services to small businesses in your rural area. In the "About Us" page, insert a good color picture of yourself and maybe even of you with your family to give prospective clients an idea of what you look like. Remember the conservative character of most small towns. A photo of a clean-cut family man will make a much better impression in a conservative town than one of a tattooed hippy with spiked hair and earrings.

On your "Contact Information" page, make sure your cell phone number is shown as the primary contact number by highlighting and bolding the numerals. You can also create a vCard from an entry in MS Outlook that includes all of your contact information. A client can just click on the hyperlink on your website that's linked to your online vCard, and it will be directly imported into their Contacts within Outlook on their computer.

The "Services" page will describe the numerous services you offer as a rural computer consultant. If you offer more than 8 of the 40 profitable computer services previously listed in this book, you will want to create groupings of the services and put them on multiple web pages. On my site, I have categorized my services under Windows Management, Consulting Services, and Website Management, with a separate web page per category, each of which gives a description and/or example that can be viewed.

To create this website, use Microsoft's FrontPage. You will probably need a good how-to book on FrontPage or you can take an online class from www.VTC.com. (As previously mentioned, this online learning service is a great source for quick-study projects for both you and your clients, which makes it well worth the $30 per month fee.) In the worst case, you can use the FrontPage Wizard and included website templates to get the first draft of your company's website online.

After you get the first version of the website designed and uploaded by using the Publish feature in FrontPage (or just by pushing it up to the hosting site via file transfer protocol), you then need to view it from multiple web browsers under various screen resolutions. Since Microsoft still has around 90 percent of the browser market covered with Internet Explorer (IE), make darn sure that your site is formatted correctly

to look good when viewed with IE. Try viewing your website also with Netscape, Firefox, and Opera. See how your new site fits on screens with the smallest monitor resolution of 800 x 600 pixels and then view it again with the most popular resolution of 1024 x 768.

When the site looks good from most platforms and resolutions, you'll need to make sure people can find it. Cover the basics by setting up the meta-tag description and key words with just the right phrases and words so that search engines and web spiders can pick them up correctly and list your site. As I mentioned before, you can use online meta-tag analyzers such as the one from www.widexl.com to help you tweak your tags for best performance.

By far the quickest way to draw new visitors to your website is by using Google AdWords (https://adwords.google.com), which is a pay-per-click advertising service that puts your customized sponsored ad on the right side of any Google results page from a search that contains your targeted key word. For a minimum budget of $1 a day, you cannot beat this deal. Watch out for other website listing and advertising vendors, since they can be expensive and troublesome.

You'll need to create your e-mail address under Webolocity's cPanel website management interface, but before you do that, make sure you enable the SpamAssassin utility to mark all incoming junk mail with the word *spam* in the subject line. This will allow you to create a single rule under Outlook or Outlook Express that can throw all tagged spam into the Deleted folder (rather than clogging up your Inbox). Make sure you have a large enough disk quota on the e-mail account so that large attachments and numerous big e-mail messages will not fill up your mailbox and reject subsequent e-mail messages.

Test the sending and receiving of the new e-mail account thoroughly not only from Outlook, but also through web-based e-mail tools such as www.mail2web.com. This free site allows you to check your e-mail in-box from any Internet-connected PC by entering your e-mail address and password.

Once you're happy with the site, your e-mail is working reliably, and all links are solid, send the URL to your colleagues, friends, and family and have them view the web pages and test them. Ask for their comments and recommendations.

With the website up, tested, and available for client viewing, you will now be able to put the website URL and your e-mail address on all materials, such as business cards, hard copy brochures, and advertising prints.

9

Home Lab and Mobile Office

The barometer for how well your new consulting business is doing will be how much you're billing per month. The next indicator is how much time you're spending on the country roads visiting client sites for sales calls, or better yet, for billable consulting projects.

The first couple of years, I spent most of my time in my home office, which became a corporate lab with shelves of hardware and software along with tables covered with computers, laptops, and surge protectors to power them all. I spent my time making business visits to develop new sales leads, creating marketing campaigns, learning new skill sets, or working on customer PC problems in my lab.

As time went on and my client list grew, I became more "mobile office" oriented, and spent the majority of the time in my vehicle rather than in the lab. During that three-year transition, I learned what was important to

have in both the home-lab and the mobile-office environment.

Your start-up business location will be your home office. Don't waste money on a storefront or rental-office space in town, since all you'll be doing is making phone calls and preparing marketing materials. All these marketing and sales projects can be conducted from your home office. Simply select a remote room within your house, an environmentally controlled garage office, or a room in a guesthouse on the property.

Home Office/Lab Recommendations

One of the most important issues here is privacy and quiet. You'll be talking to clients on both your cell phone and your landline and you need a room with a locking door or a remote office that's free of background noise from the household sounds of kids running around.

Verify that the cellular phone that you'll be using as your primary business telephone number has a good signal (of at least two bars) and will actually ring when clients call. Also make sure that you have cell-phone data connectivity so you can get voice-mail notifications, SMS messages, and e-mails sent to it. Since you will have just moved from a different area, you may initially have cellular-coverage or connectivity problems.

When we moved from Houston to Brenham, I still kept my cell phone number with the area code from Houston rather than Brenham. My cell phone service provider, Verizon Wireless, doesn't charge for long-distance calling within Texas, and since my friends and family knew my cell phone number, and I had used this number for almost ten years, I kept it after our move to the country.

That was a big mistake! When I printed my Houston cell phone number on my business cards, marketing materials, and website, new clients thought I was a Houston-based consultant trying to drum up business remotely and that I wasn't an actual resident of Washington County. After a couple of years of slow local sales growth, I realized that two things were probably holding me back: one was the Houston area code on the cell phone serving as my primary contact number, and the other was my nonrural yuppie car (a BMW).

The bottom line here is to have a primary phone number that is local, along with a vehicle that fits in well with the surroundings. In Texas, the vehicle of choice is a four-door pickup truck, and that is what I got. At the same time, I also procured a new primary phone number with a Washington County area code. Interestingly enough, after that, my local business started booming.

Your home office should have a jack for your home phone and a fax. This fax line can also serve as your primary business line if you also order call forwarding and configure it to forward calls to your business cellular phone. I had to do this because Verizon did not offer 979 area code phone numbers for their cell phones back then. For more than one month, I fought with Verizon to port a local 979 phone number to the cell phone but got nowhere. So I have kept that landline of (979) 289-2233, which costs me $20 a month, and now I just modify the call forwarding to whichever cell phone I'm carrying.

Having your primary business phone number as a local landline, with calls forwarded to your cell phone, is highly recommended. This gives you the freedom to change cellular providers, eliminates the hassle of trying to port your published rural business number, and means you avoid having to change all your marketing materials. However you configure it, just make sure that when a client calls the main phone number on your business card, the call goes to your cellular phone.

In your home office, you will want a standard desktop Windows PC with MS Outlook constantly running and receiving e-mail from your primary e-mail address. It is a good practice to keep all of your business-related e-mail messages organized in folders by either subject or date. I have e-mail messages from clients and vendors dating back to 1999. Your e-mail tool of choice should be Microsoft's Outlook. This is because Microsoft Office has the largest market and is the de facto standard. Outlook is the primary e-mail application, and it also houses contacts, a calendar, tasks, and notes. The vast majority of your commercial clients will be using Microsoft Outlook, and so should you.

Make Outlook your master business-contacts database by utilizing the Contacts feature to maintain all phone numbers, e-mail addresses, postal addresses, and contact notes of all your clients and vendors (along with your friends and family). Use the Calendar module of Outlook for scheduling your workweek and as a time sheet for tracking your billable hours. The Tasks module can help you keep track of all the things you need to do for your growing business and client projects.

The PST data file for Outlook located deep in the "Documents and Settings" directory will become one of the most important files for your business, so make sure you back it up every day. This PST file will be large, so back it up to another PC hard drive or tape backup.

You'll also need a good color printer that can handle 13" x 19" size paper (to make network maps) and a separate scanner. If you can, avoid three-in-one printer/scanner/fax devices since they often have performance problems due to complex drivers. You will also need standard home-office equipment such as a fax, paper shredder, and office supplies.

Mobile Office Recommendations

The most important tool you will use during your business day will be your cell phone. I strongly recommend you purchase the latest Palm OS/PDA smartphone that your cellular provider offers. The Palm phones are far more versatile than the BlackBerries and even the Microsoft phones due to the numerous little programs that are available for the Palm OS platform. As of the time of this writing, I use a Palm Treo 650 Smartphone branded by Verizon, which syncs up with Outlook flawlessly.

The key to your mobility is having all information in MS Outlook running on your office PC mirrored to your cellular smartphone. This way, you'll have every phone number, e-mail address, task, and calendar event at your fingertips. During the business day, you can add contacts, modify the task list, and edit calendar items, and then have all that updated information downloaded and synchronized back to Outlook on your office PC at the end of the day. This backs up the critical data on your smartphone in case of hardware failure or, God forbid, loss of your smartphone.

Depending on your state or province's cell phone usage laws, it may be mandatory to use a hands-free device to talk on your cell phone while driving. Since Texas has fewer "nanny" laws than some other states, we just have to use common sense when it comes to talking on our cell phones while driving. I recommend using a wireless Bluetooth earpiece with one-touch communications with your Bluetooth-enabled cellular phone. Once your business gets going, you will be burning up 1,500 to 2,500 minutes a month talking to your clients, vendors, and other support personnel over your cell phone, with most of that time from the inside of your vehicle. Obey the antidistraction driving laws in your state or province, use a hands-free headset or earpiece with your cell phone, and focus on the road.

As I mentioned before, choose a vehicle that will blend in well with the small-town environment you have moved into and definitely do not try to showboat. Good fuel mileage would be a major plus since you'll be putting almost as many miles per month on your car, SUV, or truck as the number of minutes on your cell phone. I average around 2,500 to 3,000 miles a month on my pickup, which requires a monthly oil change. Since you will often be transporting PCs, monitors, and other computer-networking equipment in your vehicle, make sure you have plenty of interior space.

Documenting your travels will be critical for mileage-expense deductions that can add up to $1,000 a month. I accomplish this with a small $300 GPS device from www .LandAirSea.com that plugs into my cigarette lighter, sits on my dash, and logs all my driving activities. At the end of the week, I download the business-travel data into my PC and run the Past-Track software that produces a history of activity showing all the locations I went to (graphically on the mapping software). Next, I create an activity log that I then copy and paste into an Excel spreadsheet, which produces a comprehensive mileage-expense report that no IRS agent could complain about.

The other important tool you'll need in your mobile office will be the troubleshooting laptop. This Windows XP Professional laptop should have an internal wireless network interface (802.11b/g), a CD-RW/DVD drive, and a floppy drive even if it is external. Along with Microsoft Office Professional, you will also need numerous software tools

(all of which I'll list in Chapter 10) for troubleshooting wireless and wired networks. Buy a sturdy laptop case or bag for this laptop and make sure you have room in the side pouches for the numerous cables you may need for network equipment such as Cisco routers and switches.

A couple of other things that will accompany you during the day's travels to customer sites will be your CD-ROM case and Flash/Thumb drive.

You will probably be reinstalling, repairing, or updating software, which will require a portable library of installation CD-ROMs. Bear in mind you will not be distributing or installing illegal copies of software, but you will have the need for authentic software such as Windows XP Professional and Home, Service Pack CDs, MS Office CDs, antivirus CDs, and other frequently required programs during repairs and reinstallations.

It will be obvious when clients have illegally copied software, because after a hard-drive crash, they may want you to reinstall the same CD-ROM of MS Office 2000 onto more than one PC. Do not do it! Instead, have them buy or help them buy a new legal copy from a local dealer or a valid online vendor. If the current software installation is valid but needs to sample the CD-ROM or pull some additional files from it, having the necessary software installation CD-ROM handy in your CD-ROM bag will save you time.

The Flash or Thumb drive is a great thing to have around your neck. It is there, ready to install free software such as Microsoft's Windows Defender, Spybot, or any of the other numerous software tools that are listed in Chapter 10. Spend around $100 and get one that will hold 1GB (1,000 megabytes) along with a write-protect switch to protect it from getting infected from virus-infested PCs. I got my Imation 1GB Flash drive (from www.imation.com) with a neck band, quick-release connector, and an attached rotary cap that will not get lost. You can also partition a chunk of space on your Flash drive for quick backups of critical files for your clients.

As your business develops, the focus of your needs will move from the home office to your mobile office, and these tools and methods will help you work efficiently and profitably as a rural computer consultant.

To help you make sure you've got all the basics you need to get your consulting business started, I developed the Home Office/Mobile Office checklist (see Checklist 2).

CHECKLIST 2
HOME OFFICE/MOBILE OFFICE

Home Office:	Got it?
Inkjet color printer able to handle 13" x 19" paper	
Fax machine	
Jack for office fax/phone	
Has door with lock or is remote from rest of house	
Paper shredder	
Flatbed scanner	
Standard desktop Windows PC running MS Office	
Strong cell phone signal	
Basic office supplies: paper, stapler, envelopes, etc.	
Large multicompartment binder to store receipts and tax form copies	
At least an 8-Port Ethernet switch with long patch cables	
Strong UPS (uninterruptible power supply) for desktop PC	
Plenty of power outlets from UPS or surge protectors	
Large amount of clear table space	
External USB-attached hard drive for backups	
Spare monitor, keyboard, and mouse for PC test area (used is fine)	
Mobile Office:	
CD-ROM bag and CD-ROMs of Windows, Office, and other applications for update/reload purposes	
Palm Treo Smartphone (with local area code, data connectivity, ability to sync with Outlook)	
Cell phone hands-free device such as Jabra BT500 Bluetooth headset	
USB Flash/Thumb drive with at least 1GB storage	
GPS device to log driving activities, track mileage, and locate new client locations	
Laptop computer with wireless capabilities	
Laptop case/bag with ample side pouches for cables	
Vehicle (reliable, appropriate, ample interior, good fuel mileage)	
DC/AC power adapter from cigarette lighter to 110v power	

10

Network Toolbox

Over the past six years of providing computer network consulting services as a rural computer consultant, I have accumulated an array of software utilities, programs, and suites that I call my network toolbox. This network toolbox is a collection of freeware, shareware, and evaluation copies of software that I can install on client computers to help me troubleshoot Windows problems, remove virus infestations, analyze networking issues, and examine server performance difficulties.

About the Toolbox

I keep this toolbox on CD-ROMs in a CD holder that resembles a large photo album. It holds more than 100 CD-ROMs and has a zipper for protection. Large items such as Microsoft Windows XP Service Pack 2 (weighing in at 225MB) and Server 2003 Service Pack 1 (at well over 330MB) get their own CD-ROMs. The majority of the 100-plus other utility programs fit on a single 650MB

CD-ROM, which is labeled Network Toolbox. I have used this CD-ROM multiple times a day at client sites for years, and my customers are amazed at my collection of handy tools to fix almost anything on their computers. For even quicker access in a smaller package, I have the network toolbox software saved on my 1GB Thumb/Flash drive. Keeping the Flash drive hanging around my neck allows me to leave the CD-ROM collection in my truck.

On my website at www.DeansConsulting .com (under the Company Essentials drop-down menu), there is a Toolbox page where the top 30 of these utilities are available for online access by my clients and peers. I even download and use them myself on the rare occasion that I am without my Thumb drive and CD-ROM case. Building up this battery of utilities took years of web surfing, downloading, and testing these helper programs, which I had read about on ZDNet, Download .com, or in numerous computer magazines.

There are three kinds of programs in the network toolbox: freeware, shareware, and evaluation versions, and all of them are legal to download, swap, install, and test. The freeware programs are as they seem: completely free to install and use permanently, as long as you do not try to sell them. Shareware programs are usually versions of software with a long or unlimited evaluation period and have a very low purchase cost. Evaluation software typically has a 15- to 60-day evaluation period, during which you can test it out and decide whether or not you want to formally purchase the application.

You can use all these programs for short periods, and you can use them at client sites to help you analyze computer-networking problems and usually resolve the majority of them. I did not include digital copies of my network toolbox applications with this book because it would take only one lawyer to find one clause in the EULA (end user license agreement) of one program that he or she thinks I have violated in some small way — and then the lawyer would get after me. (There are, however, web links provided on the accompanying CD-ROM.) We will talk more about dealing, or should I say not dealing, with lawyers later in this book.

One of the tools in my network toolbox you're welcome to use is "Network Metrics," which is an Excel workbook filled with network-technology information. This informational database includes items such as an IP addressing subnet conversion table, comprehensive descriptions of all types of Ethernet, distance limitations and types of DSL, and many other helpful definitions and metrics tables related to computer networking. You can find it at http://DeansConsulting.com/toolbox.htm. Since the Network Metrics workbook is an accumulation of public domain material, there are no legal issues involved, so download and check it out free of charge.

What the Toolbox Contains

Sample 3 is a table of contents of nearly one hundred of the network utilities and software programs I've gathered, tested, and used at client sites over the past several years.

You can find any of these programs easily by doing a Google search on the program's name, or by clicking on the web links provided in the Toolbox section of the CD-ROM.

Let's briefly review ten of my favorite network tools that will help you a great deal in the field.

NetPerSec is a great little utility that monitors the performance of your network interface card (NIC) and graphically displays the real-time and historical throughput rates with both downstream and upstream graphs. This is a must-have to see how fast your local- or wide-area connections are running, and it's perfect for verifying your Internet connection speed.

LView Pro is a simple and capable image editor that can manipulate, convert, compress, and crop images in JPG, BMP, TIFF, and GIF formats. This is nagware shareware that will just bug you until you pay for it. Since it is small and fast, LView Pro is great for a quick throw-down image editor when Microsoft Paint is not enough and Adobe Photoshop is too much.

NETWORK TOOLBOX

Tool Name	Description	Licensing
IamBigBrother	activity monitoring software	evaluation
eBlaster	activity monitoring software	evaluation
Acoustica	audio capture to MP3/WAV	evaluation
AutoDesk DWF Viewer	AutoCAD DWF viewer	freeware
Autodesk DWG True View	AutoCAD DWG viewer	freeware
DWG Viewer	AutoCAD DWG viewer	freeware
Data Deposit Box	automated online backup service	evaluation
AVG Anti-Virus	antivirus tool	evaluation
AVG Virus Removal	a variety of specialized tools for virus removal	freeware
Modem Spy	call recorder via modem	shareware
IdentaFone Pro	caller ID software for PC	evaluation
GreenBow VPN	client VPN software	shareware
Indeo Codec	codec software for audio and video files	freeware
EZAudit	computer hardware/software auditor	evaluation
Belarc Advisor PC Audit	computer hardware/software auditor	freeware
Net.Medic	diagnostic tool for dial-up connections	freeware
DynSite	Dynamic DNS Client	evaluation
SnipeIt!	eBay automatic sniping tool	pay per use
Delenda	file archiving tool	evaluation
GetDataBack	file recovery software	evaluation
Mozilla Firefox	free web browser	freeware
SWiSH	Flash development tools	evaluation
Imation Disk Manager	Flash drive partitioner	freeware
WS FTP	file transfer software	evaluation
LView Pro	image editor and viewer	evaluation
Hacker Tracker	hacker tracking service	subscription
Active Smart	hardware diagnostic software	evaluation
Dr. Hardware	hardware diagnostic software	evaluation
NetBrute	Windows network vulnerability testing tool	freeware
Nuzzler Basic	intrusion detection software	freeware
VisualRoute	connection testing and IP address tracing tool	evaluation
Google Earth	map and satellite image software	shareware
Microsoft Malicious Software Removal	worm removal tool	freeware
Crystal Player Professional	MPG/MPEG video player	evaluation
Intel Vtune Performance Analyzer	Windows Server 2003 performance analyzer tool	evaluation
SharePoint Services	SharePoint Services for Windows Server 2003	freeware
NetPerSec	internet connection speed and throughput monitor	freeware

PDANet	network connection tool for wireless devices	evaluation
NetDoppler	network testing tool	freeware
WhatsUp	network monitoring tool	evaluation
Orion Network Performance Monitoring	network monitoring tool	evaluation
Network Metrics	networking information database	freeware
Microsoft Baseline Security Analyzer	network security management tool	freeware
QuickBooks Online Backups	online backup service for QuickBooks and other important data	subscription
OpenOffice.org V2	open-source software version of Office Suite	freeware
4Team for Microsoft Outlook	Outlook workgroup sharing software	evaluation
WallWatcher	firewall and router data analyzer	shareware
Internet Explorer Password Recovery	password reset and recovery software	evaluation
Atomic Clock Sync	PC clock synchronizer	freeware
Adobe Reader	PDF viewing software	freeware
Win2PDF	PDF conversion software	shareware
AdSubtract	pop-up blocker and privacy software	evaluation
MSCONFIG	portable MSCONFIG.EXE for Windows 2000	freeware
Process Explorer	process diagnostics for DLL problems and leaks	freeware
Qcheck	Qcheck network performance tester	freeware
QuickShutdown	Quick Shutdown tool for Windows	freeware
QuickTime	QuickTime viewer with iTunes	shareware
Brava! Desktop	reader for a variety of document, image and CAD files	shareware
Remote Desktop Client	remote desktop client for Windows 2000 and earlier versions	freeware
Personal Folders Backup	Outlook add-in for backing up folders to PST files	freeware
PRTG	network and bandwidth use monitoring software	freeware
Qurb	anti-spam software	evaluation
Norton Removal Tool	Norton software removal tool	freeware
SAV Password Removal	special Symantec AV password removal tool	freeware
SpyHunter	spyware and adware removal software	evaluation
Spy Sweeper	spyware removal and blocking software	evaluation
Ad-Aware	spyware scanning and removal software	freeware
CWShredder	CoolWebSearch removal software	freeware
HijackThis	spyware scanning software	freeware
Windows Defender (beta)	spyware detection and removal software	freeware
Spybot — Search & Destroy	spyware detection and removal software	freeware
Advanced Subnet Calculator	automatic subnet calculation and network address division tool	freeware

SupervisionCam	remote surveillence software	shareware
Kiwi Syslogd Daemon	Syslog logging software	freeware
CRT 3.0	terminal/console software	freeware
Tftpd32	TFTP server program	freeware
Advanced USB Port Monitor 2.0.1	USB port analysis tool	shareware
Office 2003 Viewers	viewers for Office suite programs	freeware
Virtual Bouncer Remover	Virtual Bouncer removal tool	freeware
VCleaner	virus cleaner	freeware
VNC for Windows	Virtual Network Computing remote access software	freeware/ evaluation
CamSurveillance	webcam surveillance software	shareware/ evaluation
SubmitWolf PRO	website promotion tool	evaluation
RegCleaner	Windows registry cleaner	freeware
Windows Server 2003	Windows Server 2003 R2	evaluation
WinSockFix	Windows WinSock repair tool	freeware
Windows XP	Windows XP Service Pack 2	freeware
WinZip	file compression software	evaluation
NetStumbler	wireless network security testing tool	shareware
Symantec Removal Tools	removal programs for specific worms and viruses	freeware
ZoneAlarm	firewall software	freeware/ evaluation

GetDataBack is a must-have to be able to recover deleted files and retrieve data from reformatted or even damaged hard drives. The evaluation version will show you the lost files available for recovery, but you will have to purchase the software to get those files back. It is well worth it for the NTFS and FAT32 recovery bundle, and it will pay for itself the first time you recover some lost or damaged files for a client.

MS Windows Defender was created originally by Giant Software, which was bought by Microsoft, who now distributes this great antispyware utility free of charge. I guess Microsoft figures that since they created the spyware industry due to the vulnerabilities in Internet Explorer, they had to offer a no-charge solution to their problem. The beta version works well and will only get better.

Belarc Advisor is a nifty computer hardware- and software-auditing tool that is free from Belarc.com. This is especially helpful when you first sit down at a new troubled PC and need to know what software is running on what kind of hardware. The first audited item I look for is the amount of installed RAM and the number of SIMM slots used and still available. Though the licensing on this software is not for commercial use, it is perfect for your home-user clients.

OpenOffice is a look-alike for Microsoft's Office suite that is available from an offshoot of Sun Microsystems called OpenOffice.org.

The "Writer" program can read and write MS Word .DOC–formatted files and responds just like Word. MS Excel is mimicked by the "Calc" spreadsheet application, which can both read and write .XLS files. The "Base" application serves the purpose of the MS Access database program, and the "Impress" module looks just like MS PowerPoint, reading and writing PPT files. The OpenOffice suite is free and it's a great substitute for those illegally copied versions of MS Office 2000, which you must remove if you find them.

AVG Anti-Virus is my top choice for fighting and preventing viruses on Windows workstations. Because McAfee and Norton antivirus programs have gotten so big, slow, and expensive, I started implementing AVG Anti-Virus for all my clients in 2004. The cost per PC per year is down to $11, and the program is much more efficient and reliable. AVG originally offered a free version of 7.0 for home users but replaced it with a 30-day trial in 2005.

RegCleaner is an excellent free utility that finds legacy and faulty entries in the Windows Registry and cleans them up. I was nervous the first couple of times I used RegCleaner, as it was free and developed by one guy in a faraway country, but it came highly rated on Download.com. RegCleaner has worked flawlessly and has helped me resolve complicated problems and eliminate ghosts in clients' computers.

WhatsUp is my favorite network management tool. It monitors entities on your network, has a graphical mapping interface, and can notify you of failed nodes via e-mail or pager. Ipswitch.com offers a 30-day evaluation, which can be handy at new sites. I recommend the purchase of WhatsUp for use on your troubleshooting laptop to monitor networks in the field. We used this program in my Compaq days back in 1998 to monitor a campus network supporting more than 12,000 nodes — and had no problems.

NetStumbler is one of the tools you will want to have when troubleshooting wireless LANs or performing security reviews for clients. This free program is great for sniffing out wireless coverage zones and listing critical wireless information such as the SSID, channel choice, and security settings. Try it out in your own urban or suburban neighborhood and see how many wireless networks there are around your home.

A good rural computer consultant always carries a potent network toolbox. Use this list to start your own network toolbox by downloading the latest versions of these helpful utilities and applications. Begin researching solutions to the problems you are seeing at client sites and build upon this collection by going to www.Download.com and www.ZDNet.com.

11

Initial Marketing Campaign

By this time, you will have been saving money, creating a list of potential clients, and preparing to pull the trigger to start making an income as a rural computer consultant. The next big step is to begin the initial marketing campaign and start selling your services.

The whole point of this campaign is to get your name out in the community and to make your business offerings known. Because they'll have heard about you, companies in your new rural area will call and give you a shout when they have a computer problem or a hot networking project that needs some local expertise.

Your start-up marketing campaign will have five phases:

1. Marketing materials
2. Local newspaper print ad
3. Direct-mail project
4. Cold-calling

5. On-site sales calls

I've designed these five phases to be performed in the order in which they're listed. That way, you'll create all the materials you'll need first, then get your company's name and service offerings broadcast on a wide basis, then to a targeted audience, and, finally, you'll be directly contacting that potential client pool.

Marketing Materials

The first phase of your marketing plan is to develop three sets of marketing materials:

- Basic business cards
- CD-ROM business cards
- Company brochure (trifold)

Basic business cards

There are many business-card services online that can help you produce a professional-looking card in minutes and have them shipped to you the next day. One good site I have used often is www.CardConnection.com. There are even some sites that offer free cards if you just pay the shipping. On your card, be sure to use the postal address of your home to show the locals that you actually live in the community. Also, as the primary telephone number, use your cell phone number or a local landline phone number (forwarded to your cell phone). Be sure the card includes your website URL and e-mail address. Sample 4 is my business card for Deans Consulting. It lists my services and all my contact information.

CD-ROM business cards

After producing your basic set of business cards, the next step is to create a CD-ROM business card (see Sample 5) with an auto-start Flash presentation including moving text, pictures, music, and maybe even a video. This will really get a prospective client's attention.

In 2001, I attended a BICSI seminar and trade show where I first saw vendors handing out small CD-ROM business cards that played a Flash presentation of their company's products and services. After being shocked at the $3 to $5 per card cost from commercial CD-ROM business-card producers, I set out to make them myself. A few months later, I found a great application called SWiSH that easily produced Flash presentations for around $50 from www.SWiSHzone.com.

The online media vendor www.cdrom2go.com sold rectangular blank CD-ROMs, glossy labels, vinyl sleeves, and a label-applicator device for around $100.

It only took me a couple of weeks to develop my own Flash presentation and burn it onto CD-ROM business cards. These multimedia business cards, which cost me around $0.75 each, automatically starts playing when inserted into the CD player of any Windows computer.

This Flash presentation takes over the whole screen, and background music begins to play. I picked a song from a favorite Clint Eastwood movie that had a low royalty fee.

SAMPLE 4
BUSINESS CARD

www.DeansConsulting.com

Computer Networking

*Your Washington County
Computer Consultant*

979.289.2233

Windows Tuning & Upgrades	Security Audits
Server 2003 Conversions	PDA Configurations
Website Design	Network Troubleshooting
Voice Over IP	Wireless LAN & WAN Design

Email: John@DeansConsulting.com   USPS: 6206 Ganske Rd, Burton, TX 77835

CD-ROM BUSINESS CARD

My presentation shows the prospective client my background, my services, and finally my contact information. The final screen thanks them for viewing and has a hyperlink to my website. I've included my CD-ROM business card presentation (without the music) on the CD that comes with this book.

These CD-ROM business cards really get prospective clients' attention with just the look of them, and if they actually take the time to play them on their PCs, they will be very impressed. I highly recommend you take the time to create your own set of multimedia CD-ROM business cards to send, along with your trifold brochure, to sales leads when you conduct your first direct-mail project. As I'll discuss later, these CD-ROM business cards can make your cold-calling a whole lot easier.

Promotional brochure

The next marketing item you need to create after you've got your basic and/or CD-ROM business cards is an informative, single-page brochure. It should include a picture of you, a brief history of your professional background, and a detailed list of all the computer and consulting services you offer.

These trifold brochures can be mailed out during your direct-mailing campaign and hand delivered to clients during your first sales call at the customer's site. Sample 6 shows my early brochure, both the front and back of the single-sheet trifold.

Local Newspaper Print Ad

The local newspaper is the place to start your initial marketing campaign if you want to be introduced to the small-town businesses in your area. The goal here is to make potential clients aware of your new company's name and the computer services you offer, and to provide all your contact information. Sample 7 is the newspaper ad I ran in every Sunday edition of the *Brenham Banner-Press* for three months.

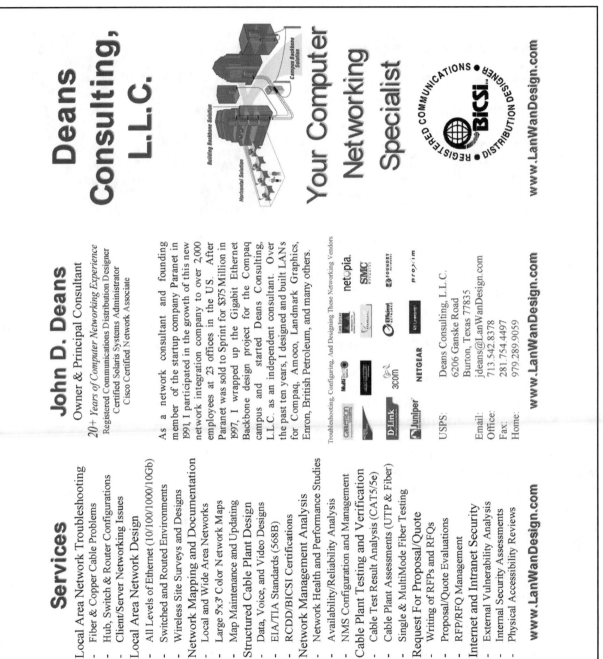

Deans Consulting, L.L.C.

Your Computer Networking Specialist

www.LanWanDesign.com

John D. Deans
Owner & Principal Consultant

20+ Years of Computer Networking Experience
Registered Communications Distribution Designer
Certified Solaris Systems Administrator
Cisco Certified Network Associate

As a network consultant and founding member of the startup company Paranet in 1991, I participated in the growth of this new network integration company to over 2,000 employees at 23 offices in the US. After Paranet was sold to Sprint for $375 Million in 1997, I wrapped up the Gigabit Ethernet Backbone design project for the Compaq campus and started Deans Consulting, L.L.C. as an independent consultant. Over the past ten years, I designed and built LANs for Compaq, Amoco, Landmark Graphics, Enron, British Petroleum, and many others.

Troubleshooting, Configuring, And Designing These Networking Vendors

netopia.
SMC
FOUNDRY
Pro×IM
Efficient NETWORKS
Lucent
NETGEAR
MultiTech
3Com
D-Link
Juniper
Cabletron Systems

USPS:	Deans Consulting, L.L.C.
	6206 Ganske Road
	Burton, Texas 77835
Email:	jdeans@LanWanDesign.com
Office:	713.542.8378
Fax:	281.754.4497
Home:	979.289.9059

www.LanWanDesign.com

Services

- Local Area Network Troubleshooting
  - Fiber & Copper Cable Problems
  - Hub, Switch & Router Configurations
  - Client/Server Networking Issues
- Local Area Network Design
  - All Levels of Ethernet (10/100/1000/10Gb)
  - Switched and Routed Environments
  - Wireless Site Surveys and Designs
- Network Mapping and Documentation
  - Local and Wide Area Networks
  - Large 5x3 Color Network Maps
  - Map Maintenance and Updating
- Structured Cable Plant Design
  - Data, Voice, and Video Designs
  - EIA/TIA Standards (568B)
  - RCDD/BICSI Certifications
- Network Management Analysis
  - Network Health and Performance Studies
  - Availability/Reliability Analysis
  - NMS Configuration and Management
- Cable Plant Testing and Verification
  - Cable Test Result Analysis (CAT5/5e)
  - Cable Plant Assessments (UTP & Fiber)
  - Single & MultiMode Fiber Testing
- Request For Proposal/Quote
  - Writing of RFPs and RFQs
  - Proposal/Quote Evaluations
  - RFP/RFQ Management
- Internet and Intranet Security
  - External Vulnerability Analysis
  - Internal Security Assessments
  - Physical Accessibility Reviews

www.LanWanDesign.com

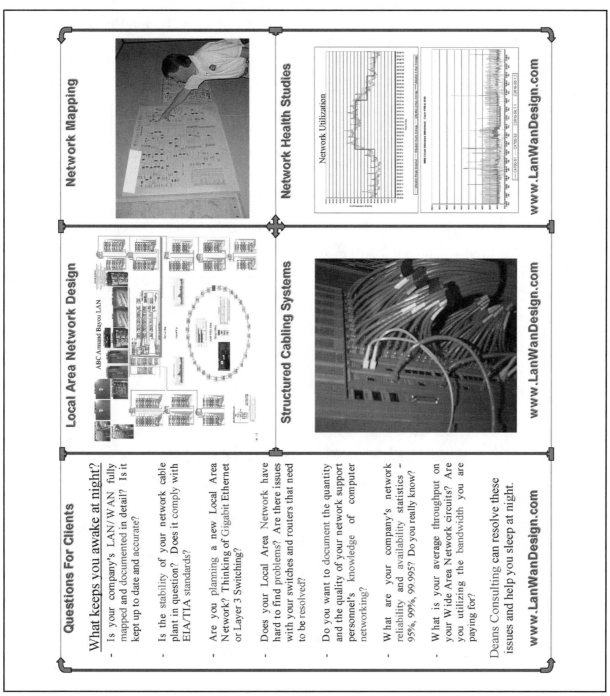

Network Mapping

Network Health Studies

Network Utilization

www.LanWanDesign.com

Local Area Network Design

ABC Armand Bayou LAN

Structured Cabling Systems

www.LanWanDesign.com

Questions For Clients

What keeps you awake at night?

- Is your company's LAN/WAN fully mapped and documented in detail? Is it kept up to date and accurate?

- Is the stability of your network cable plant in question? Does it comply with EIA/TIA standards?

- Are you planning a new Local Area Network? Thinking of Gigabit Ethernet or Layer 3 Switching?

- Does your Local Area Network have hard to find problems? Are there issues with your switches and routers that need to be resolved?

- Do you want to document the quantity and the quality of your network support personnel's knowledge of computer networking?

- What are your company's network reliability and availability statistics – 95%, 99%, 99.995%? Do you really know?

- What is your average throughput on your Wide Area Network circuits? Are you utilizing the bandwidth you are paying for?

Deans Consulting can resolve these issues and help you sleep at night.

www.LanWanDesign.com

This ad clearly showed that I was a local consultant whose interests and efforts were focused on Washington County, in which the town of Brenham is the county seat. My experience and certifications were mentioned, and several rhetorical questions were included to provoke thought and get the readers' attention. The ad had all my contact information and ran only on Sundays, since that is when the majority of people have some spare time to actually read the paper. You may notice that my primary contact number now has a Washington County area code rather than the 713 Houston area code that appeared on older marketing materials.

Instead of running a classified ad amid the jumble of garage-sale and used-car ads, I paid to have the ad placed in the middle of the first section of the newspaper alongside the news articles, for better readership. The cost of the 4" x 2" ad was around $20 per week and was well worth the $240 I spent to have it run for three months of Sundays.

Though I only got a few calls from people who said they were calling me because they had read my newspaper ad, I found out later, during my cold-calling, that most had noticed my ad and were keeping me in mind.

Direct-Mail Project

At this point, you will have a basic set of business cards, an informative single-page trifold brochure, and perhaps a set of multimedia CD-ROM business cards. And you will have also taken out a newspaper ad. After the ad has run for a couple of weeks, it's time to conduct your direct-mail project, which is the first focused step to making direct contact with potential clients.

SAMPLE 7
NEWSPAPER AD

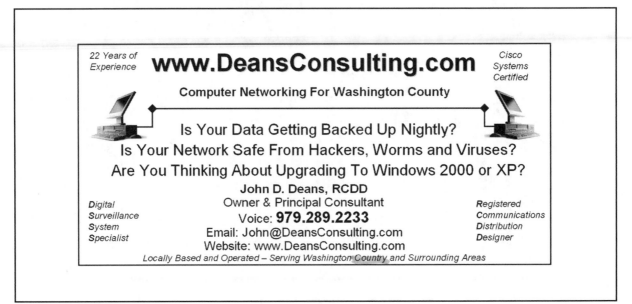

In Chapter 7, you prepared an Excel spreadsheet of prospects to cold-call. Right now, though, this spreadsheet will serve as the lead list for this direct-mail project. Look up any mailing addresses for companies you only have a phone number for. And then prepare a simple cover letter and enclose it with a brochure and a CD-ROM business card for each prospect. Sample 8 is the direct-mail cover letter I sent out that really got things going.

When you stuff the envelopes, make sure you sign each letter and then handwrite the address on the outside of the envelope. A handwritten address on the envelope will help separate your letter from junk mail. You might also think about buying a rubber stamp that says "Confidential" and a red-colored inkpad to stamp each envelope next to the address. This stamp increases the chances that it will be opened only by the addressee. Mail out the first ten envelopes, wait a week, and then begin your cold-calling to those ten prospects.

Cold-Calling

After a week has passed, it's time for the hard part: cold-calling.

I had to buy a couple of books on this topic because like most people, I didn't like the thought of calling up complete strangers and trying to sell them something. But I hit on a formula that made it easier for me. When I called a prospect and they answered the phone, I'd introduce myself and, first of all, ask them if they'd had a chance to view my CD-ROM business-card presentation. This really helped break the ice, since most of my prospects had never seen one before. The ones that played the CD-ROM and viewed the presentation were impressed and were already familiar with my company's name and the computer services I offered.

When you start your cold-calling, you'll be working from the same lead list spreadsheet you used for the direct-mail campaign. You'll start with the first ten names of people who should have received your sales package that week. Before you call any of them, put together a script and rehearse it well so you don't sound like you're reading it. In fact, you should have it memorized so that you don't stumble and say "uh" and "um" the first ten seconds of the call. Sound happy, energetic, and very polite, with "Yes, Ma'am," "Please," and "Thank You" throughout your conversation. If you schedule your calls between 8 a.m. and 10 a.m., you'll have the best odds of reaching your primary contact when they are likely still in a good enough mood to listen to your sales pitch.

Just like I did, use the question, "Did you receive the CD-ROM business card I mailed you this week along with my brochure?" to break the ice and get things going. Since the majority of these small-town business people will actually open the handwritten letter marked "Confidential," it's likely that your contact will have at least looked at your sales package. Your chances of them opening it are also increased if they noticed your newspaper ad running over the past few weeks.

Fall back on leaving a voice message only after two failed attempts to talk directly to your contact. If you do leave a voice mail and your contact is not on vacation or away from the office for an extended period, wait for a couple of days and try one more call. If after three calls and a voice mail you are unable to

SAMPLE 8
DIRECT-MAIL COVER LETTER

www.DeansConsulting.com

Computer Networking

CONTACT NAME
COMPANY
ADDRESS
CITY, STATE, ZIP

Your Local Computer Professional

Dear CONTACT NAME,

I would like to introduce myself and the Computer Networking Services that Deans Consulting offers clients of Washington County. The enclosed E-Card overviews consulting areas that include network troubleshooting, computer performance tuning, Windows XP/2003 upgrades, network security and wireless LAN configurations. Local clients include: Appel Dodge, Ant Street Inn, Collier Construction, TFE Company, Del Sol Foods, Houston Unlimited, Texas Broadband, Heritage Texas County Properties, Dr. Reeves Braces, Dr. Paul LaRoche III D.D.S., Jim Lee Realty, Round Top Real Estate, San Bernard Electrical Cooperative, Brenham Presbyterian Church, Brenham Veterinarian Hospital, Larry Arnie CPA and many more.

The enclosed E-Card (CDROM) has a FLASH presentation overview of my company. This dynamic E-Card will start on any Windows PC. Just place the E-Card in the CD tray on your PC or laptop, and it will automatically start within 30 seconds. It looks strange, but it is completely safe for your CDROM player.

Call me about any computer problems or new projects!

Thank you,

John D. Deans, RCDD
Owner & Principal Consultant
Deans Consulting, L.L.C.
6206 Ganske Road, Burton, TX 77835
Email: John@DeansConsulting.com
979.289.2233

Please View The Deans Consulting E-Card Presentation on CDROM

22 Years of Experience

Cisco Systems Certified

talk to your contact, put this one aside and go on to the next lead. To keep all the information organized for follow-up efforts, use the marketing contact list spreadsheet to keep track of whom you called, when you called, and what response you got. (See Sample 9.)

When you do get your contact on the phone, you will want to find out if they are having any current computer problems, software issues, or upcoming networking projects that you could possibly assist them with at this time.

The way you go about this is to simply ask questions, for example, "How stable are your computers?" "Are you happy with the performance of your computer network?" or "If your PC or server's hard drive died right now, how much data would you lose?" I can almost guarantee they will bring up at least one problem they are currently experiencing, and it will be your job to have a solution ready.

If there is the slightest bit of interest, ask to schedule an appointment with them as soon as possible at their site. Then you'll be ready to make your first on-site sales call.

On-Site Sales Calls

Once you get through the physical doorway of a client's office, you are home free, since they most likely will have something for you to fix, troubleshoot, or consult about.

Make the sales meeting on time, if not five minutes early, and present yourself enthusiastically and professionally. Dress appropriately for your business and in attire that is common for the area. I almost got laughed out of the first sales call I made when I drove up in my BMW and walked into the client site in my slacks, tie, and loafers. The country gentleman chuckled and advised me that trying to sell something wearing a suit and driving a yuppie-mobile would not get me far around here. The next week, I traded in my Dockers and loafers for

SAMPLE 9
MARKETING CONTACT LIST

Company	Card Mailed	Cold-Called	Status	Contact Name	Address 1	Town/City	State/Prov	Zip Code/Postal Code	Telephone	Fax

blue jeans and boots. Soon after that, the BMW was traded in for a Dodge Crew Cab pickup truck. The difference in first impressions was astonishing.

Have a look at Checklist 3, Marketing Campaign Materials. Use the form you'll find on the CD-ROM accompanying this book to help you stay on track when you launch your initial marketing campaign.

CHECKLIST 3
MARKETING CAMPAIGN MATERIALS

Use this checklist when creating your marketing materials to ensure your materials contain all the necessary information. As you complete each piece, check it off.

Basic business cards	
Include:	
Company name	
Your name	
Contact information (i.e., address, cell phone, fax, e-mail)	
Website URL	
List of services	
Completed:	

CD-ROM business card	
Include:	
Pictures	
Moving text	
Video	
Your background and brief overview of your experience	
Your services	
Label with all information from basic business card	
Completed:	

Company brochure (trifold)	
Include:	
Company name	
Photograph of yourself	
Summary of professional background	
Detailed list of services	
Contact information (i.e., address, cell phone, fax, e-mail)	
Website URL	
Completed:	

CHECKLIST 3 — CONTINUED

Newspaper ad	
Include:	
Company name	
Your name	
Thought-provoking questions that indicate how you can help the prospective client	
Your certifications and years of experience	
Contact information (i.e., address, cell phone, fax, e-mail)	
Website URL	
A statement that you are locally based	
Completed:	

Cover letter for direct-mail campaign	
Include:	
Company name	
Your name	
Contact information (i.e., address, cell phone, fax, e-mail)	
Website URL	
Statement introducing yourself and your company	
Statement encouraging reader to view Flash presentation on enclosed CD-ROM business card	
Invitation to reader to call you anytime about computer problems or projects	
Make sure you handwrite all addresses on outside of envelope	
Enclose:	
CD-ROM business card	
Company brochure	
Completed:	

PART 5

GROWING THE BUSINESS

12

Self-Employment Discipline

Once you make the commitment, start up your own consulting business, and have to rely on your self-generated income for survival, the word "initiative" will have a whole new meaning for you. No one is going to knock on your door or seek out your phone number and request consulting services without a strong, positive, and consistent effort by you and you alone. So do not expect your cell phone to start ringing just because you ran a newspaper ad for a couple of weeks or left a few voice mails for potential clients. You need to adopt a professional salesperson's mentality and the ability to aggressively yet politely pursue consulting opportunities.

The Initiative Fire

During the initial weeks and months, you'll have plenty of downtime with no client activity, calls, or inquiries. You will have to stay positive and put yourself on a regular work schedule by getting up early, getting dressed for work, and reporting to your home office, even if it's just down the hall. It will be tempting to sleep late or do household projects, but keep one thing in mind to hold your feet to the fire: fear of failure.

Though it sounds negative, the fear of not making enough money to keep the new company in the black is the kind of carrot-and-stick mentality that motivates many people. Many have tried and many have died (business-wise), but the ones who succeed are those who stay focused, positive, active, and motivated. You've got to be a self-starter and want to do this business with all your might. The small-business winners provide their own carrot, while the stick of money-driven realities is not far behind them.

To be one of those driven small-business winners, you will have to keep the following in mind:

- You alone will put in the massive effort required to execute your business plan and to develop all marketing materials and get them out to the best sales leads in your area.

- You alone will make those dreaded cold calls with a cheerful and enthusiastic demeanor to get an appointment with those potential clients.

- You alone will have to understand what the client wants and provide a solution, whether that is a quick fix for a half-hour of billable time or a comprehensive project plan addressing multiple computer-related issues.

- You alone will have to constantly learn new technologies, applications, protocols, and solutions to the latest digital problems and provide results in a timely and efficient manner.

- You alone will verify the job was done correctly and make darn sure the client is not only satisfied, but also impressed with your performance and professionalism.

- You alone will accurately track the time and resources you spend serving that client and invoice him or her fairly with a consistent and clear billing process.

- You alone will collect the generated revenue and divvy it up to pay the company's taxes, expenses, and finally your salary.

- You alone will get up early the next day and do it all over again and love every minute of it!

This all may sound melodramatic, but you'll understand once you start getting responses from sales leads, make on-site sales calls, close business deals on a handshake, perform the work, and finally open that mailbox at the end of your driveway and see that first check.

Time Management

Time management also takes self-employment discipline. During those initial slow times, you can be tweaking the marketing materials, adding new leads to your direct-mail list, or learning new skill sets so that you can offer a wider range of computer services. One of your early goals must be to stay busy. You'll know you've had a good day when you lay your head down at night and think about all the different little things you accomplished that day that will ultimately generate more business for you.

Once business picks up, time management will take on a whole new meaning. This is especially true when multiple clients call for your services the same day, if not the same hour. Though it may seem far off at this point, eventually you will have the problem of having too many clients request your assistance at one time. You will have to prioritize them by order of urgency and severity.

First, you should give your attention to the client who has the most users negatively affected by the computer problem, even if you have to reschedule others. For example, if you are on the way to a client site to do a Windows upgrade, and another client calls with a server supporting 20-plus users that has crashed, you will, of course, reschedule the upgrade project and race to the downed server site.

The big issue is to live and work by the following rule:

Do What You Promised To Do When You Promised To Do It!

This means DO NOT be late! Since every businessperson has a cell phone and voice mail, there is no excuse for being late to an appointment without notifying the client before the time you are due to arrive. Small-town business people may not have the obsessive-compulsive expectations of big-city clients, but they want their time to be respected and must be able to rely on you to deliver your services on time.

But there's a flip side to cell phones: they can become a crutch for your tardiness. Do not let that happen. We can get spoiled easily with our instant communications capabilities, so keep in mind that just because you called at 8:55 a.m. to notify the client you will not make your 9:00 a.m. appointment, it doesn't mean that all is peachy-keen. You will still not be there at the agreed-upon time, which the client probably made time for in a busy calendar.

Exhaustive Customer Service

As a rural computer consultant, you must be disciplined not just in showing up for appointments on time, but also in answering the phone, returning voice mails, and replying to e-mails. Fourteen years ago, I was the first consultant at Paranet to have a cell phone with which to better service my customers. My Paranet co-workers thought I was showing off at first, but when they saw me solving client problems and billing time while driving around in my car, they quickly changed their tune.

If you want to make your rural clients happy, do one simple thing: answer your cell phone when a client calls you! Do not ignore it when it rings or let it go to voice mail. Of course, there will be exceptions, such as when you're in one-on-one meetings, but that will be rare. Keep your cell phone physically on you and make sure it has a loud ring tone so you'll hear it no matter where you are. If your environment is too noisy for you to hear it ring, put your cell phone on vibrate and stick it in your front pocket so you'll feel it.

In case some of your client calls do go to your cell-phone voice mail, make sure you keep your voice-mail greeting short. Simply say, "Thank you for calling XXX Consulting. Leave a message, and I'll get right back to you." Check the messages often enough to not have a voice-mail notification flag active, and also because some cell phones don't show this flag if you have more than one voice-mail message waiting. Make it a goal to generally return voice mails within 15 minutes and always within an hour.

One of the reasons I recommended a stationary desktop PC for the home office is so it can be constantly receiving e-mail messages into MS Outlook. It is also important to leave this computer on and logged in continuously in order to provide daily backups of your critical business data to another computer, tape drive, or online backup service such as Data Deposit Box. You will also want remote access to your home office PC via GoToMyPC.com, which is simpler than VNC, Remote Desktop, or pcAnywhere. Though remote access services currently cost approximately $14 a month paid annually, it is worth it to be able to access your already downloaded e-mail from any Internet-connected computer.

Check your e-mail regularly at least three to five times a day. Since most cell phones now have SMS (short message service) capabilities, you can provide this alternate e-mail address so your clients can send short messages directly to your cell phone, which will enable you to reply back instantly.

If you have messages that you cannot reply to instantly, flag them with a "Follow Up" icon to mark them for action as soon as possible. Create Outlook folders named after your clients and move your e-mail messages to the appropriate folder so that you always maintain a complete record of correspondence with each client.

The golden rule for your company e-mail is to respond to every e-mail message with at least some sort of reply and helpful information. This diligence is just as important as showing up on time, answering your cell phone, and returning calls left on voice mail.

As a rural computer consultant, your self-employment discipline is absolutely critical to your success. Stay on top of your appointments, immediately answer your clients' calls, religiously check your voice mail, and reply to all client e-mails.

Every person thinking of becoming an independent consultant needs to read *Who Moved My Cheese?* by Dr. Spencer Johnson. If you are like the ever-positive and self-motivated mice Sniff and Scurry, then this business is for you. For those others of you who refuse to see the writing on the office wall and fail to react and adapt to the ever-changing markets and industries, you may be imitating the other two characters, Hem and Haw. Read Dr. Johnson's best-selling book and you'll see what I mean.

13

Continued Marketing and Word of Mouth

Once you get those first few clients, you'll feel a boost of confidence and realize that this business is actually going to work. Treat those initial clients with the most focused customer service you have ever imagined. If you miss their calls, return them within minutes. When you get their e-mails, call them in addition to e-mailing a reply. Inundate them with friendly, fast, and thorough computer service. This exhaustive customer service, along with other promotional projects, will enable you to continue growing your client list.

There are all kinds of ways to promote your business, but the most effective are those that spring from your own small-town environment. Those methods are the focus of this chapter.

The All-Powerful Word of Mouth

When you acquire your first few clients, nurture them. That will be the beginning of the all-important word-of-mouth marketing that will account for more than 90 percent of your future clientele. The start-up marketing campaign discussed in Chapter 11 will get you those first few. Your main goal as a rural computer consultant is to make those first clients so happy with your service and impressed with your skill sets that they'll brag about you to their business friends and other local townspeople.

Those first very satisfied clients will bring you the next five clients. Pamper those five with your outstanding customer service, enthusiastic attitude, free services, and vast computer knowledge, and they will link you up with your next ten clients.

The all-powerful word of mouth will spread your name throughout the countryside in a matter of days, for better or for worse. This is why it's absolutely critical that you not disappoint in any form or fashion while serving the first clients you acquire through your direct-mail and cold-call campaign. There will not be a second chance.

Small-town talk burns like wildfire. It can make you or break you, so be sure it spreads in a positive way.

Network with Local Organizations

One of the neat things about living in a small rural community is that you will often see the people you work for at various events and everyday places. You will run into your clients at the grocery store. You may see them on Sundays at the same church. And living in Brenham, I quickly learned not to honk at anyone for minor roadway annoyances like I did on a daily basis in Houston's miserable traffic. The odds were too high that it could be a future client who would remember my vehicle, or even a current customer who would recognize my face. In big cities, it is very rare to see a client randomly in traffic, but in small rural towns it is commonplace to see many people you work for while driving from site to site.

You can put these reoccurring happenstance meetings to good use by giving current or prospective clients the chance to get to know you better personally.

Your goal should be to be visible and positive in the public's eye. Expand your small-town presence by participating in local groups, events, and activities. Earlier I had recommended joining the local chamber of commerce, not only to obtain the membership list to use as a marketing tool, but also because it's a good organization to belong to and it will boost your visibility. Keep an eye on their calendar mailings, which will list events and activities that you can attend. Our Washington County Chamber of Commerce has a monthly "After Hours"

networking session hosted by one of the member businesses. These professional get-togethers for small-business people are great meeting environments where you can introduce yourself, casually explain what you do, and offer a business card if you sense other members' interest in your services. Attend the ribbon-cutting ceremonies that most chambers conduct and tactfully ask the new business if they are having any computer-related problems or challenges.

As your client list grows and your family makes new friends in your new town, you may get an invitation to attend a luncheon of the local Rotary Club. Jump at this opportunity. The first Rotary Club was established more than 100 years ago, and Rotary Clubs make up the Rotary International organization, which is a private professional group that has more than 32,000 clubs in more than 200 countries worldwide. Their motto of "Service Above Self" explains their goal of providing goodwill services for the local community and charity projects all over the world.

Since one has to be invited to attend a meeting as a guest, I was fortunate that one of my favorite clients asked me to join him for lunch at a Rotary meeting back in 2004. I was quite impressed by meeting the 60 other business leaders and professionals that were the cream of the crop of free enterprise in Washington County. I was also surprised and pleased to see a few of my other clients there as members of the club. After attending several of these Rotary luncheons as my client's guest, he put my name and professional history in an application for my membership. A few months later, I was formally accepted, made a full member, and have been attending the weekly Thursday Rotary meetings at noon like clockwork.

The Rotary presence is so strong here in Washington County that there is also a Brenham Rotary Club, which is roughly the same size as the Washington County Club. Members from both clubs occasionally attend each other's luncheons and events. There may be some competition between the two clubs, but it all is good natured and to the betterment of both groups.

Being a member of the Rotary Club allows me to meet the leaders of the community and the heads of the smallest to the largest companies in our rural county. Everyone is very friendly, and it is incredibly easy to meet and interact with potential clients on a weekly basis. You'll find yourself sitting around a six-seat table with a varied set of Rotary members every week, and they'll start asking you computer questions during lunch as soon as they find out about your consulting business. Within the first few months of attending Rotary meetings, I gained several new clients without having to directly sell or pitch to them.

There are other organizations such as the Kiwanis Club and the Lions Club that may have different membership requirements and goals but have similar networking value. Try to make yourself available and express interest to members of all these clubs to get invited and involved.

Local Charity Events, Donations, and Sponsorships

There are other ways to make sure the local business community is aware of your company and familiar with the services you provide, and being open to donation or sponsorship requests from local charities is one of the best. Of course, your first priority here is to provide financial assistance to a good charitable cause, but it will not hurt your business if you get exposure and name placement as a result of your donation.

Often charities and sponsored events run newspaper and radio ads and have large banners at their events displaying the names of companies that donated to their cause. Find out the donation amount required to get public recognition in one or more media. Many small-town events will put your name in the paper for even just a $100 donation or sponsorship. You can also offer to sponsor the area Little League or soccer organization by providing the funds for uniforms with your company name on them.

Keep in mind that the majority of your current and soon-to-be clients have spouses that are active in local charities and kids that will participate in sponsored athletic activities. As your company name becomes more visible as a consistent donor and sponsor of these community projects, the small-business people will be more open to trying out your services. Other good groups to support are the local chapter of the Boy Scouts, Girls Scouts, and Boys and Girls Clubs of America (and Canada), and the local children's museum and heritage museum.

You'll find you can produce both goodwill and new business opportunities for yourself by providing funding through your company to the local community's charities and sponsored activities.

Write a Newspaper Column

As a rural computer consultant, you will be experiencing, researching, troubleshooting, and resolving many computer problems that relate to various fields of the technology industry. One great way to provide an excellent service to your local rural community (while providing your company with outstanding public exposure) is to volunteer to write a weekly technology column for the local town or county newspaper. You'll be doing this on your own nonbillable time, but you'll get a tenfold return by way of advertising and business contacts.

This article-writing project will take time to develop and sell, along with weekly effort to author an original 500- to 1,000-word column. Back in early 2004, I put together a new column proposal to the only newspaper in Washington County, the *Brenham Banner-Press*. After getting to know the managing editor, I scheduled a meeting and delivered a presentation to him on how I wanted to start writing a new information-technology column for the *Brenham Banner-Press*. During the presentation, I gave him both printed and electronic copies of the initial article, already written. After a couple of months of discussions with the paper's owner about article content and my intent to focus on local computer-related issues, I got the chance to start writing for the *Brenham Banner-Press* weekend edition on a unpaid basis beginning in April of 2004. I was determined to be in the weekend edition since it gets the most attention and the highest readership. Sample 10 is my proposal to the *Brenham Banner-Press* that got my column started.

You may think there will not be enough subject matter for a 1,000-word article on a weekly basis, but you'll be surprised how topic rich the IT industry is and how your column can be written to address local issues. Sample 11 is a list of the topics covered in my column in the *Brenham Banner-Press* over a seven-month period. A complete list of my column with links is provided on the CD-ROM.

Since my first article, published in April of 2004, I have e-mailed a 1,000-plus word article every week without fail. Within two months of the appearance of my first IT column, I was receiving very positive feedback, and new clients began contacting me. They obtained my contact information from the last sentence running in every article:

> *John Deans of DeansConsulting.com is a Brenham-area computer-networking consultant who can be reached at 979.289.2233 or John@DeansConsulting .com for your questions and comments.*

The managing editor told me that the paper's circulation increased after my column started running, and that they had readers who had lost the prior weekend paper drop by the newspaper's office to purchase copies just to read my articles.

I try to write the articles in the same way I'd talk to clients to help them understand a technology issue. I keep my descriptions and explanations simple and easy to understand. I define any acronyms I use, if I use any at all. I also try to keep my columns interesting by using a conservative political tone to reflect my right-wing viewpoints. This right-leaning feel to my column reflects the political makeup of Washington County — 75 percent of the county voted for President George W. Bush, and every elected county official is a Republican. This tone helps spice up the column and keeps it from being a dull series of technology articles.

NEWSPAPER COLUMN PROPOSAL

To:	*Brenham Banner-Press*
From:	John D. Deans — Computer Networking Consultant
Subject:	Helpful Computer Tips Column Proposal

My name is John Deans, a local computer networking consultant, and I am proposing to write a weekly column for the *Brenham Banner-Press* that will provide helpful and realistic tips, ideas, and guidance through the maze of computers, software, hardware, and networking for the residents and companies of Washington County.

Starting in the early 1980s, I went from computer operator, to programmer, to analyst. In the 1990s, I designed, built, and managed computer networks for companies such as Amoco, British Petroleum, Compaq Computer, and many more. By 1998, I had enough of Houston and moved my wife and kids to our ranch just west of Brenham and started Deans Consulting in 1999. That was the best decision I ever made! My goal has been to deliver enterprise-level experience and service to small businesses in the Washington County area. The people around here are great, and I thoroughly love my job serving both commercial and residential clients. With more than 30 active clients in the Washington County area, I have developed a full-time computer consulting practice delivering prompt and proactive support.

The proposed column will serve both the small business client and the home computer user, providing them with useful information to better manage their computer resources. My 23 years of experience have enabled me to implement real-world processes that ensure a stable, secure, and robust computer environment. In other words, I make it work right. I have been writing articles for magazines since the late 1980s and I have attached a few of the major ones with this proposal. I will be looking at general issues that affect all computers, along with others that are specific to our area of Washington County.

The Bottom Line: I am proposing to write a weekly column for the *Brenham Banner-Press*, delivering my expertise to the readers.

- The column is to be published in the Sunday edition, acknowledging the author, John Deans

That's it! No financial compensation is requested. It will be a strong positive for the *Brenham Banner-Press* to deliver computer tips, troubleshooting techniques, and computer help to the people and businesses of Washington County. Attached is the first article for the column, titled "When to Retire Your Computer."

NEWSPAPER COLUMN TOPICS

Date	Subject
May 7, 2006	MS Update Problems
April 30, 2006	MS OneCare
April 23, 2006	Tracking Your Tee
April 16, 2006	Prepare for the Worst
April 9, 2006	Google Earth
April 2, 2006	IE Favorites
March 26, 2006	Office 2007
March 19, 2006	Blogging
March 12, 2006	Treo 700w
March 5, 2006	Digital Voting
February 26, 2006	TomTomGO
February 19, 2006	HDD Management
February 12, 2006	Online Surveys
February 6, 2006	Windows XP Tuneup
January 29, 2006	Slingbox
January 22, 2006	High-Tech Millionaires
January 18, 2006	Apple IPod
January 9, 2006	2005 Review and Update
January 1, 2006	Extreme Makeover — Home Edition Network
December 25, 2005	Opening Digital Gifts
December 18, 2005	Computer Sound
December 11, 2005	RFID
December 4, 2005	Christmas List
November 27, 2005	PDF Files
November 20, 2005	Google
November 13, 2005	MySpace.Com
November 6, 2005	Cyber Warfare
October 30, 2005	UN Internet Takeover
October 23, 2005	Online Computer Support
October 16, 2005	Home Computer Support

Since my picture runs with the weekly column, it wasn't long before locals I'd never met started coming up to me in cafés and stores to tell me how much they enjoyed my articles. With newfound small-town popularity generated by my column, along with growing and strongly positive word of mouth, the calls from new clients with computer projects and troubleshooting opportunities skyrocketed. In late 2004, I had to send out an e-mail to my existing client base saying that to continue serving them at the high level of quality they were used to, I was suspending acceptance of new clients for at least six months.

Putting in all this effort to produce a weekly computer column for the local newspaper may seem like a big investment, but it will be your most important marketing project and can generate numerous business opportunities for you. It's well worth it.

Speaking Engagements with Community Groups

Once you start writing your IT column, community groups, business organizations, and even breakfast prayer clubs will start calling you to speak at their luncheons, breakfast meetings, and official gatherings. Over the past couple of years, I've given numerous talks at meetings for such groups at their request. Since these presentations are excellent marketing opportunities, I don't even think of charging for them. I bring my laptop and projector to make PowerPoint-aided presentations. These talks are usually only 20 to 30 minutes long, and the groups range in size from 5 to 50 people.

When you're invited to speak to a group, try to make the topic as interesting as possible by including some local color and local examples. Remember that these technology talks are not sales calls, so do not talk about the services you offer or try to pitch yourself to the audience. All you need to do is deliver important and useful information on issues such as fighting viruses, worms, hackers, and spyware. Deliver the talk impartially and enthusiastically, and the people who made up your audience will seek you out later for possible consulting opportunities.

Free Advertising with Giveaways

I deliver shirts and calendars to my clients as promotional and marketing giveaways, much like the giveaways large companies hand out at technology trade shows. The shirts are nice long-sleeve, button-down dress shirts from Lands' End with the Deans Consulting logo on them. They cost around $25 each and are great marketing items to drop off to your primary clients. Many times I have seen my clients wearing my Deans Consulting shirts around town, which is great advertising.

Once a year (in December), I create a Deans Consulting calendar for the next year. I create a large Excel spreadsheet, then make it into a calendar with my company logo, contact information, and a question for each month. Questions include, "Are your backups running every day?" "Do you have hard-to-find networking problems?" and "How safe are you from hackers and viruses?" I plot these 3' x 4' custom calendars out on an HP DesignJet 755 color plotter, which can be bought used on eBay now for a fraction of what I paid for it back in 2000. Clients love these calendars, and they attract a lot of attention throughout the year hanging on their walls. For the last three years, I've plotted and distributed more than 100 Deans Consulting calendars to my clients.

No-Charge Services

Over the past few years, I've learned that providing special services free of charge to my clients is one of the most effective marketing tactics there is. Offering no-cost services to your clients provides them with multiple benefits and can lead to billable trouble-shooting sessions and future projects for you.

By providing these special services, you're trying to help your clients become more proactive in managing their computer environments. It is commonplace for most small companies to be in a perpetually reactive mode, performing quick fixes and making temporary Band-Aid repairs without addressing the root of a problem. As rural computer consultants, we can take action to help our clients resolve issues before they become major difficulties. I'll spend the rest of the chapter describing my three favorite no-charge services.

Data-backup monitoring

One of the services I offer clients whose backup systems I have built or reconfigured is monitoring of their daily data backups. I do this by configuring the e-mail notification capabilities in tape-backup software applications like TapeWare and Backup Executive to send backup logs to me. The first things I look for in my e-mail in-box each morning are the 12 e-mail messages automatically sent to me from 12 different client sites, each containing the logs to that client's nightly tape-backup job. If I get less than 12 messages in the morning, I know

that one or more has failed or has gotten hung up — which, of course, requires my billable intervention.

This daily verification routine has helped keep the critical backup processes running smoothly at those 12 client sites for years now. Since it only takes me a couple of minutes a day, I do not charge those clients for this service. However, I do bill them when I have to visit the site to change a tape, restart a process, or clean the tape drive. It may seem trivial to change a tape, but when a bad one stops the backup process for days, if not weeks, all the data for the whole company is at risk.

Most mornings when I check the backup logs (which all arrive by 6 a.m.), I simply scan the Outlook Inbox and glance at the size of the e-mail messages. When there's a problem, the size of the message is either far less or much more than the normal 10KB message. If I spot a problem with the size of any message, I open it to investigate what abnormality occurred in the backup job to cause a smaller or larger log file.

Another task I perform on the tape-backup log files is to search the messages for words like "skipped" or "locked" to verify that all files are being properly backed up. I do this to ensure nothing is happening at night at the clients' sites that could be holding files open and keeping them from being backed up to tape. All it takes is one critical database file skipped for one backup cycle, and a hard drive failure will cause the total loss of that vital file forever.

When I first propose to implement a new backup solution or reconfigure an existing one, I volunteer to monitor the backup jobs on a daily basis at no charge. The clients love this, it gets me back to the site to resolve tape- and file-related problems that eventually develop at all sites, and it helps me sleep at night knowing my clients' data is protected.

Many of my smaller client sites lack formal servers with a tape drive to perform the backups. Instead, these clusters of workstations push their data via Microsoft Backup to the shared drive of a central workstation acting as the workgroup backup server. To remotely check on these PC-to-PC backups, I configure a remote-access portal into the PC with either Remote Desktop or VNC to view the creation times on the backup files. Since I have configured all these daily automatic backups under Windows Scheduled Tasks, they should have the same date on the archive files. If one or more has not been updated in a day or more, I know I have to make a billable visit to the client's site to resolve the problem. The resolution could involve something simple such as reminding the user of the workstation not getting backed up to leave the PC powered up and logged in. Other resolutions might be more complex, and could involve an analysis of possible computer problems, network-throughput problems, or hardware instabilities. All of these activities are billable. Watching the backup activities can call you into action without you having to get a call from the client.

Whenever I need to intervene on account of a backup problem and have to visit the client's site, I notify them that their backup procedure has encountered a problem, and I am there to resolve it to protect their company's data integrity. My clients are as happy to pay me to resolve the problems immediately as I am happy to monitor for free the backup logs via my e-mail.

Network management system

I recommend that you purchase the WhatsUp network monitoring package. This affordable NMS (network management system) can be quite valuable to you as a rural computer consultant because it will enable you to offer another free service to your clients. Years ago, I took one of my older laptops, cleaned it up, upgraded it to XP Professional, and installed the WhatsUp version I bought back in 2001 from Ipswitch.com. For several years now, that laptop running WhatsUp has served as my NMS to monitor the Internet connections of more than 30 clients.

The WhatsUp display shows a grid of green icons representing the client sites whose Internet links are up and ping-able. When any of those client sites lose their connection (due to their DSL or wireless ISP having problems), WhatsUp turns that client icon red and notifies me in an audible voice that a link has dropped. Since I am out of the office the vast majority of the time, it also sends a short e-mail message to my cell phone, immediately telling me of the downed connection.

I maintain this NMS system and provide 24x7x365 monitoring of these 30-plus client sites at no charge. This network watchdog of mine provides me the comfort of knowing all is well with my clients' networks. It also gives me the timely alerts I need to contact a client or visit a site when their Internet connection drops.

Over the past five years, connectivity to the Internet has become vital to most of my clients. Some even have all their sales, inventory, and accounting on web-based ASPs (application service providers) that are absolutely dependent on a stable Internet connection. Without a reliable ISP, they cannot do business. When these Internet-uptime-dependent client links drop, and I am alerted via text message, I am able to call the client within a few minutes of the event, and they are astonished at my quick response. I'm also notified when the site comes back, which means I can call the client and let them know that all is OK. This is helpful, too, since there are times when people are just sitting around thinking their web access is still unavailable when in fact it's been back for hours.

Watching your client's backup activities and monitoring their Internet connections at no charge is a good deal for all concerned: both of these free services help your clients' computing environments become more proactive and put you in position to take billable action when problems arise.

No-charge loaners

As the years go by, you will acquire multiple PCs, printers, scanners, and even projectors along with other computer equipment. It is a good idea to hang on to these assets, maintain them, and have them ready to loan out to a client in need of a fast replacement.

One item that is not often used but very handy to own is an LCD projector. You'll need one for presentations at client sites, but you'll find it has other uses. There have been multiple occasions when clients of mine needed projectors because they either did not have one, or if they did, it was broken or already in use. I was happy to drop mine off and set it up for them at no cost, since it would just be sitting on my shelf collecting dust. Goodwill gestures like this get overwhelming positive response from clients, and your good deed will come back to you many times over in good ways.

Likewise, keep a spare PC with MS Office loaded and ready to go in case a client loses a critical workstation due to hardware failure. You can bill for the time that you transfer the data and install any special programs needed, but let them use your PC for free instead of charging them a rental fee. You'll have protected them from the loss of productivity they'd otherwise have experienced. They will love you for that, and more business will come your way soon.

The bad thing about small towns is that the bad word spreads fast. The good thing about small towns is that the good word spreads pretty quickly also. Your free monitoring services and no-charge loaner program will go over big in your small town, which will help make you a popular and profitable rural computer consultant.

14

Estimating, Project Scoping, and Deal Making

Most of the time, the first visit you make to a new client will be to help him or her fix a problem. So once you get your foot in the door, the next step is to listen to the client closely to understand what the client really means rather than just what he or she is saying. You will want to gain a full comprehension of the computing problems the company is experiencing, and get a feel for where the client is on the reactive to proactive scale. Make sure to bring a pen and notebook to take notes on problem specifics, and at the same time scribble down possible projects you can recommend later that will help the client become more proactive — projects such as better backup procedures, updated antivirus software, and upgrading Windows.

Initial Troubleshooting Deals

Before you make any recommendations for future projects, make sure you focus on the problem or problems you were brought in to discuss in the first place. Exceptions here would be if the client has a server-crashing problem and has not been doing backups correctly, or at all. (The first thing to do in this case, before touching the server, is to back up the user data correctly and completely. *Never trust the client's assurance that the data is backed up*. Always view the backup-software configuration and recent backup logs and verify that the client actually changed the tapes or other backup media.)

If the new client has multiple problems with network performance involving multiple computers, he or she may request a fixed price or at least a firm estimate on how much it will take to solve the problem. At that point, you'll need to explain to the client that it is very difficult to quote the exact cost due to the numerous variables involved. I usually handle this by explaining that I will strategically and methodically troubleshoot the problem one level at a time and fix any related issue that could be contributing to the overall situation.

As you eliminate each possibility and fix problems along the way, give the client hourly status reports so he or she feels involved in the process and understands that you have to analyze and work the problem through one issue at a time. A client will feel much more comfortable after a billable six-hour debugging session if you keep him or her informed of what you've tried, what you've found, what you've fixed, and what you are going to look at next based on what you've seen.

Sometimes, however, you may be brought in to fix a simple problem like bringing five PCs up to the latest version of an antivirus program. In cases like this, you can give your client a pretty accurate estimate for the job after you sit at each of the PCs and see what shape they're in, hardware- and software-wise. If the virus definitions for the existing antivirus software have not been updated in months or the antivirus software is non-existent, you'll want to build some additional time into your estimate to remove the viruses that most likely already infest the computers.

A good rule of thumb to stick to when putting together a quick estimate is to come up with the amount of time you think the job will actually take, and then add another 25 percent to give yourself some breathing room. If you think it really will take just two hours, tell the client you estimate the problem can be fixed in two-and-a-half hours. This way, if you're right, and it does take just two hours, you will look like a champ for coming in under your estimate. If it goes the other way, you still have some buffer time

before you exceed the estimated cost the client agreed to originally.

Sometimes you'll encounter other problems and issues not immediately apparent or not disclosed to you by the client, and it blows your estimate all to heck. At this point, you'll want to sit down with the client and explain how the situation has changed due to these new problems or the previously unknown issues that you've encountered. This is also when you'll need to present your new, higher estimate.

The key here is to keep the client informed on an hourly or incremental basis so the client feels comfortable with a new computer person — you — working in his or her environment. The client wants to know that he or she is included in resolving the problem and that things are getting accomplished as the billable hours tick away.

Comprehensive Scope of Work (SOW)

For larger, more complex jobs, a simple time estimate will not be enough. For situations such as this, you'll need to create a comprehensive scope of work document.

You'll be doing this on occasions when you're brought in and given a whole list of projects a client wants performed on his or her computer network. Take good notes and listen intently for any indications that there may be other problems unknown to your new client but which also may need to be resolved in order for you to successfully complete the original list of projects. After you write down the client's project agenda, make sure you walk the network, view the infrastructure, and eyeball critical entities such as the servers, routers, and switches.

Do not give your client a best-guess estimate while you are there at his or her office. Instead, tell the client you will get back to him or her tomorrow after you put sharp pencil to paper, do some analysis, and develop a strategic project plan to accomplish the requested goals. Take your notes back to your home office and give yourself some time to digest all that you saw and were told. Then, start putting together your scope of work (SOW).

A scope of work is nothing more than a simple Excel spreadsheet that helps you to compose all the steps that will be necessary to accomplish each phase of the project. I use a simple SOW spreadsheet format that lists the project steps along with the labor, hardware, and software resources required.

Sample 12 shows a multiproject SOW that was accepted by one of my clients and that was successfully implemented within the SOW estimates. (You will find a blank Excel version of the document on the CD-ROM that came with this book.)

You will want to show the subtotals on a per-task and per-project level for your estimated billable hourly costs along with hardware, software, and any subcontracted work such as computer cabling. Make sure you clearly state that the numbers in your SOW are *estimates* and not exact quotes or a fixed-price deal.

Group the projects together and separate them with subtotals and a blank line. Next you will want to sort the projects by priority and put the most critical project at the top, with the next most important project below that one, and so on. This way, the client can view the list and costs from the most important project down to the least critical and plan and forecast the estimated expenditure. It takes effort and thought to put together a comprehensive SOW, so make sure you take your time and sleep on it overnight to see if you remember anything the next day that you may have left out.

You may be pondering if you should bill for the time spent visiting the site and compiling the SOW. The rule of thumb I use is if the creation of the SOW results from the first on-site sales call visit, the time visiting the site and compiling the SOW is *not* billable. However, if an existing client comes up with a laundry list of new things to be done that requires a SOW, then I do charge him or her for it as general consulting.

After you have created, pondered, and reviewed your SOW spreadsheet (which is the meat of the project proposal), you then will want to compose a simple cover letter that has some generic verbiage to lay out the ground rules for your professional role. These ground rules must state that sales taxes and other expenses will be charged over and above the SOW estimates. This is not a contract but rather a written statement laying out your intentions to best serve your new client. You will not have to get a signature or have it reviewed by a lawyer.

Sample 13 shows the cover letter I usually attach to the front of the SOW.

I usually present the SOW to the client a day or two after the initial consultation, review it with him or her task by task, and get a verbal verification on which project the client would like to proceed, if not all of them.

SCOPE OF WORK (SOW)

Local Network Migration — Task Descriptions	Estimated hours	$ per hour	Consulting fee	Hardware costs	Software costs	Project total
Upgrade of router/firewall and back office switch	0.50	$100.00	$50.00	$150.00		
Cost Estimate Totals	**0.50**		**$50.00**	**$150.00**	**$-**	**$200.00**

Antivirus — Task Descriptions	Estimated hours	$ per hour	Consulting fee	Hardware costs	Software costs	Project total
Removal of all existing antivirus systems, installation and configuration of AVG Anti-virus, scanning and removal of any viruses found	1.00	$100.00	$100.00		$125.00	
Cost Estimate Totals	**1.00**		**$100.00**	**$-**	**$125.00**	**$225.00**

PC Upgrades/Replacements — Task Descriptions	Estimated hours	$ per hour	Consulting fee	Hardware costs	Software costs	Project total
Replacement of Alice's PC (PII)	1.50	$100.00	$150.00	$1,100.00	$300.00	
Replacement of Nancy's PC (PIII-450MHz)	1.50	$100.00	$150.00	$1,100.00	$300.00	
Upgrade of Dick's PC from WIN2K w/256MB to WinXP	2.00	$100.00	$200.00	$125.00	$200.00	
Upgrade of Tina's PC to XPSPII and 512MB	1.00	$100.00	$100.00	$125.00		
Upgrade of Tim's PC to XPSPII and 512MB	1.00	$100.00	$100.00	$125.00		
Replacement of Kellie's rotating monitor with LCD swivel	0.50	$100.00	$50.00	$500.00		
Cost Estimate Totals	**7.50**		**$750.00**	**$3,075.00**	**$800.00**	**$4,625.00**

MS Windows 2003 SBE Server — Task Descriptions	Estimated hours	$ per hour	Consulting fee	Hardware costs	Software costs	Project total
Purchase/install/configure MS Windows 2003 SBE Server	4.00	$100.00	$400.00	$4,000.00		
Conversion of clients/file to Active Directory and new server	3.00	$100.00	$300.00			
Configuration of e-mail and shared calendars	2.00	$100.00	$200.00			
Testing and verification	1.00	$100.00	$100.00			
Cost Estimate Totals	**10.00**		**$1,000.00**	**$4,000.00**	**$-**	**$5,000.00**

Online/Offsite Backups — Task Descriptions	Estimated hours	$ per hour	Consulting fee	Hardware costs	Software costs	Project total
Configuration of offsite/online backup for critical files	0.75	$100.00	$75.00			
Testing and verification	0.25	$100.00	$25.00			
Cost Estimate Totals	**1.00**		**$100.00**	**$-**	**$-**	**$100.00**

TOTALS			$2,000.00	$7,225.00	$925.00	$10,150.00

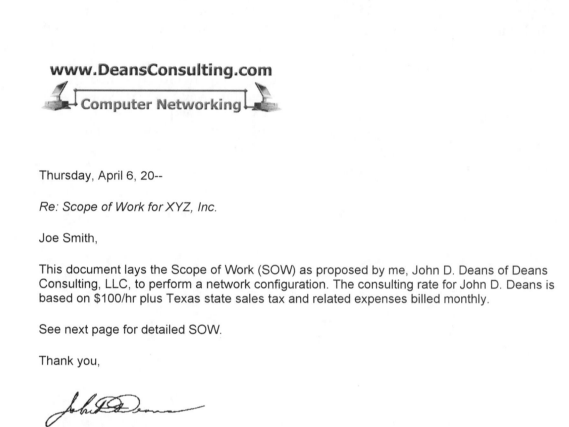

www.DeansConsulting.com
Computer Networking

Thursday, April 6, 20--

Re: Scope of Work for XYZ, Inc.

Joe Smith,

This document lays the Scope of Work (SOW) as proposed by me, John D. Deans of Deans Consulting, LLC, to perform a network configuration. The consulting rate for John D. Deans is based on $100/hr plus Texas state sales tax and related expenses billed monthly.

See next page for detailed SOW.

Thank you,

John D. Deans, RCDD
Owner & Principal Consultant

Client Handling for Best Results

I have put together some SOW documents that covered a dozen projects totaling more than $10,000, which can shock a new client. If you find yourself in this situation, tell your client that he or she does not have to implement all projects at the same time and incur the total cost all at once. Explain that you can help him or her accomplish one project at a time, starting with the most critical at the top of the list. The new client will be more open to committing to all projects if the client knows that the projects can be implemented over a number of weeks or even months.

If you author a comprehensive SOW that matches the multiple projects your client discussed with you, you've created a good roadmap to help your new client migrate his or her computing environment from a reactive to a more proactive mode. This will also go a long way toward keeping your client's expectations realistic and ensuring that the client remains satisfied as you complete each project on his or her list.

15

Financial Management of a Growing Consulting Business

One of the many hats you will wear as a rural computer consultant is an accountant's visor. You will manage the money trail from tracking your billable time to creating invoices, collecting checks, depositing funds, paying the required taxes, and finally cutting yourself a paycheck. You also need to learn to manage your business's cash flow cycle so that you never find yourself without enough money to cover all your expenses, even if you have a lean month. Financial management is the topic of this chapter.

Tracking and Billing

Before you can send out an invoice, you will have to consistently track and accurately enter your time and materials into QuickBooks. I must stress again that you should start up your consulting company with QuickBooks rather than limping along with homegrown Excel spreadsheets. Go back and reread the accounting configuration section in Chapter

8 if you have not set up QuickBooks by this point.

You need a system for accurately tracking your time. When you arrive at a client site for a billable troubleshooting session or scheduled project, your time clock starts as you enter the door. This is where your PDA smartphone comes in very handy.

I've found it useful to establish a three-character acronym for each client. For example, Collier Construction Company is CCC. So when I walk in Collier's office to work on a computer problem, I glance at the time on my Treo 650 Smartphone (which is always accurate since it is synchronized with the Verizon cellular network), open the calendar application, and enter CCC at the appointment start time. After the deed is done, their problem has been fixed, and I am walking back to my truck, I again check my Treo's time and enter the number of hours next to the CCC entry. Just before I leave the Collier site, I also adjust the CCC appointment end time. By the end of a busy day, I may have five to ten site entries all with exact start and end times, with the amount of billable hours next to the client name abbreviation (e.g., CCC 1.25).

From the beginning, I have always billed my time by quarter-hour increments. If I have to round, I usually round up, since I do not charge mileage expenses back to the client. The minimum charge for a site visit is 0.25 of an hour. I have debated with myself for years about increasing the minimum site visit charge to 0.5 hours, but so many times, I am in and out of a site after making a five-minute fix, and I'd feel a bit guilty charging 30 minutes of billable time for five minutes of work.

Part of the beauty of consulting in a small rural town is that you can get to the majority of your clients in less than ten minutes. Sometimes I'll hit a dozen client sites in a single day. Those quick quarter-hour billable visits can add up by the end of a busy day. The idea here is to consistently log your time on your smartphone so you can transfer it into your time sheet in QuickBooks at the end of every day. Never wait until the next day to enter your billable time and task information, since the details of what you did the day before will begin to fade.

When you sit down at the day's end to bring up the calendar application on your smartphone, start at the beginning of the day and enter the client-visit information along with the descriptive details of what you did there and how long it took you to do it. Avoid just putting "troubleshooting" as a task description under the notes section in the QuickBooks time sheet. Use detailed descriptions, including clients' names, project tasks, and problem resolutions. Put as much meat into the time sheet as you can, so when it comes time at the end of the month to create the invoice, the client will have an extraordinary amount of text to explain all that you did for his or her company during that time. The more detail you give the client, the less questioning and doubt you will receive from the client concerning your invoices.

Some of my invoices to my big clients after a busy month will be multiple pages long with hundreds of words describing each visit and accomplishment. I have seen a client open my large, multipage bill, look at the dense and very descriptive invoice (with sometimes multiple lines of text per billable item), and sit back saying, "Wow, you've been busy!" Being impressed by the large amount of detail, many clients cut me a check right on the spot. Sample 14 shows the kind of detail my invoices contain.

When you buy software or hardware for the client, make sure you log it into QuickBooks and bill it to the proper client with the appropriate markup. As soon as I buy an item at the computer store or Wal-Mart, I immediately scribble the client abbreviation on the receipt. The same goes for when I purchase equipment online through eBay or from an Internet-based vendor: I print the e-mailed receipt and write whom I bought it for on the printout. At the end of the day when I am entering my billable time into QuickBooks, I also input the items I purchased for clients according to the receipts from the stores I went to or the e-mail messages from the online vendors.

SAMPLE 14
DETAILED INVOICE

www.DeansConsulting.com
Computer Networking
6202 Ganske Road
Burton, Texas 77835

Invoice

Date	12/31/2005
Invoice #	2005-1571

PAID

Bill To

COMPANY
CONTACT NAME
ADDRESS
CITY, STATE, ZIP

Voice: 979.289.2233 - Fax: 281.754.4497
Email: John@DeansConsulting.com
Federal Tax ID: 99-9999999
Texas LLC Charter: XXXXXX-XX
Texas Sales Tax Permit: 9-99-9999999-9

Date	Item Code	Description	Quantity	Price Each	Amount
12/1/2005	Configuration	Staging and configuration of Steve's new Acer laptop - 31 Windows updates, AVG Antivirus install, MS AntiSpyware install, MS Windows 2003 Pro Install, Acrobat Reader 7.0 install, and other tuning tasks	0.75	100.00	75.00T
11/29/2005	Software	MS Frontpage 2003 for Steve	1.00	115.00	115.00T
12/2/2005	Configuration	Data and program migration from Steve's old PC to new Acer laptop	1.50	100.00	150.00T
12/7/2005	Configuration	Installation of evaluation WorkGroupShare software on Artex workgroup server	0.50	100.00	50.00T
12/7/2005	Troubleshooting	Troubleshooting and resolution of Andy's PC that lost its AVG antivirus which then got the Bagel virus with over 300 infected files	0.25	100.00	25.00T
12/7/2005	Configuration	Configuration of Robert's PC to have a fresh profile with his username on Windows and P2000	0.50	100.00	50.00T
12/7/2005	Configuration	Configuration of three workstations with shared calendar, contacts, tasks and notes via WorkGroupShare	1.25	100.00	125.00T
12/8/2005	Configuration	Configuration of remaining 7 PC with WorkGroupShare	1.50	100.00	150.00T
12/8/2005	Consulting	Training of Steve on Frontpage and updating website	0.25	100.00	25.00
12/8/2005	Configuration	Conversion of 3 users from Outlook Express to Outlook	0.25	100.00	25.00T
12/8/2005	Configuration	Website configurations	0.25	100.00	25.00T
12/12/2005	Troubleshooting	Troubleshooting and resolution of Email problem for Angus	0.25	100.00	25.00T
12/12/2005	Troubleshooting	Troubleshooting problem with WorkGroupShare server	0.50	100.00	50.00T
12/12/2005	Configuration	Performance configuration with WorkGroupShare settings	0.50	100.00	50.00T
12/12/2005	Consulting	Consulting with Mariana with Quickbooks and GoToMyPC.com	0.25	100.00	25.00
12/12/2005	Consulting	Consulting with Steve about website	0.25	100.00	25.00
12/12/2005	Troubleshooting	Troubleshooting Bluetooth problem	0.25	100.00	25.00T
12/14/2005	Troubleshooting	Troubleshooting P2000 PO authorization issue	0.75	100.00	75.00T
12/14/2005	Troubleshooting	Troubleshooting Skype issue	0.25	100.00	25.00T
12/14/2005	Consulting	Training Mariana on GoToMyPC.com	0.25	100.00	25.00
12/15/2005	Configuration	Website configuration - newsletter page and navigation to 2 other new pages along with formatting of 12 pictures for placement	1.00	100.00	100.00T
12/19/2005	Configuration	Pictures configurations on website	0.25	100.00	25.00T
12/19/2005	Consulting	Consulting and training Steve on Website authoring	0.50	100.00	50.00
12/22/2005	Troubleshooting	Troubleshooting printer and P2000 issues	0.50	100.00	50.00T
12/22/2005	Consulting	Consulting Steve on website authoring with picture thumbnails	0.50	100.00	50.00
12/24/2005	Configuration	Conversion of 12/30/05 Newsletters from Publisher to PDF	0.25	100.00	25.00T
12/24/2005	Configuration	Configuration of 12/30/05 newsletters to website	0.25	100.00	25.00T
12/31/2005	Email/Website Hosti...	Website Hosting by Deans Consulting and Beachcomber.net	1.00	15.00	15.00T

30+ Days Late

Subtotal	$1,480.00
Sales Tax (8.25%)	$105.60
Subtotal	$1,585.60
Payments/Credits	$-1,585.60
Balance Due	$0.00

After entering your billable time and purchased items into QuickBooks each evening, it will be time to create or update the invoices of the clients you served that day. While you're in the invoices module, you will click on the Time/Costs button, which will bring up the "Billable Time and Costs" screen. At this point, you will be able to choose the items and time entries for that day to now be included in the invoice. This is also when you will adjust the price for the items you purchased for clients with a fair markup.

I cannot stress enough how important it is to do this accounting work on a daily basis. Get into the habit of entering the day's activities into QuickBooks each evening while all the things you did are fresh in your head. Trust me on this one — you will not remember the same amount of detail the next day.

There'll be times when you'll perform a task that isn't billable because you are fixing something again that you didn't fix right the first time. Go ahead and enter those items into QuickBooks with the word "nonbillable" in the notes section of the activity, enter the actual time spent fixing again, and then make sure you enter a zero billable rate so the item charge is nil. This way, the client will see what you did on the invoice and feel good about it since you did not charge him or her for it. These nonbillable entries can also include the free services that you provide (such as data backup and network management monitoring) as we discussed in Chapter 13.

On the last day of the month, carefully review all invoices to verify there are no duplicate items, missing billable activities, or items you paid for that you forgot to enter.

One thing you do not want to do is bill a client next month for things you forgot to include in this month's invoice. Double- and triple-check the invoices *before* you mail them out, since inaccurate invoices can spoil a good client relationship quickly. On the terms of the invoice select "Net 30" so the due date will show as 30 days from the invoice date. You will be surprised that the vast majority of your small-town clients will send you a check within two to three weeks, and a decent percentage will send you a check within the first week of mailing out the invoices. Mail out all the invoices on the first day of the month so they will arrive at the client sites at the same time.

Collecting Payment

Before I focused all my efforts on Washington County, I had a particularly bad experience trying to collect payment from a client. I was taking part-time consulting jobs from a firm in Houston that shall remain nameless. With a written agreement, the company subcontracted me to troubleshoot networking-problems and perform network-health studies for a few clients, whom the company billed at a healthy markup.

After I had earned the company $12,000 in billable time from their clients, about $8,000 was due to me. I started getting nervous after the second month had gone by without a check from them. In the third month, I leaned heavily on a former Paranet colleague who was working full time there, and got him to pay $4K of their debt to me.

After the fourth month, I went to their office and lobbied for another $1,000. By that time they had declared bankruptcy, so I just held on to one of the nice laptops they had loaned me earlier in the project as collateral until they paid me the last $3,000. The company was dissolved by the end of that year, and I was lucky to collect what I did, since many other vendors were left holding even larger empty bags.

That experience convinced me to explore the possibility of not dealing with Houston-based companies and their 60-day or longer payouts.

Ever since my Paranet days, I have had a business policy governing payment: "If the client is not happy with the work I have performed for him or her, the client does not have to pay." All I ask from the client is the opportunity to set things right and resolve the problem. Just like my old Paranet boss, Mike Holthouse, taught us back in the 1990s, do the right thing for the client every time. If you keep your clients happy, collecting the money from them will be no problem. Over the past five years, I have sent out a couple thousand invoices to more than one hundred clients and have had very few problems collecting from those invoices.

As I mentioned earlier in this book, all business agreements with my clients are verbal contracts — handshake deals. They are sometimes based on a preceding scope of work (SOW) that was agreed to by the client. After all the deliverables specified in the SOW have been met, it usually goes into wait-for-the-call mode. I am also at this point waiting for the check. The upside of these old-fashioned handshake deals in the country is that the business arrangement is backed by your and your client's good word.

The downside of this handshake deal is that you have little or no legal recourse if the client decides not to pay you. Since I despise most lawyers, and prefer to solve problems on my own, this restricted legal avenue is just fine with me. There are ways you can still get a client to pay you without resorting to lawyers, and that's what I'm talking about here.

For instance, it can be worth it to check out a client's payment history before you actually start doing business with the client. In the beginning you will be hungry for clients and will pretty much take any business that presents itself. As time goes on and your client list grows, you will have the option of being more discriminating, and may actually choose whether or not you'll accept a new client. Once you reach that point, you'll be able to learn about a prospective new client before you make any commitment to him or her. Remember, the small-town talk can go both ways, and you can use it yourself to research a prospective client to see if that person pays slowly or not at all. One good source to check with is the local computer store or even a competing computer consultant. If a company has wronged one of them, be wary of that same company and think twice before investing much time in them.

If you do, however, get snookered and have a few hundred or even a few thousand owed to you in outstanding invoices with a client, you'll need to start a collection process, and this process can best be described as "patient yet persistent." My basic collection process after 30 days have passed and no check has arrived is first to make a polite call to the accounts payable department, inquire if the department actually received my invoice, and then ask what the status is on the payment. The majority of the time, the invoice was just forgotten about or misplaced, and the accounts person ends up cutting me a check that week. Sometimes clients get cash-strapped, and may wait to pay bills until after their own clients pay them.

After sixty days of nonpayment have passed, I pay the client a visit to politely request they cut me a check if at all possible. Your physical presence can be more of a convincer at this point, and it works better than a nagging e-mail or phone call.

Since I have been serving only Washington County, no more than a couple of clients have gone more than 90 days late, with one going bankrupt and another just paying very slowly. I was able to collect about 75 percent of the total the bankrupt company owed me by sweet-talking the person in accounts payable into paying me $100 a month for a few months before the company filed for Chapter 11 protection. The other slow payer stretched me out for several months but finally paid me off grudgingly, even though the client loved my work. I fired this client after the last check cleared.

Always be polite, but also be persistent and contact slow-paying clients on a regular basis to inquire about payment and collect at least a portion of the balance on a monthly basis. The slower they pay, the less incentive I have to put more time and effort down their one-way pipeline. In other words, if they again need my computer services and they still haven't finished paying me for the last job, there is less of a chance I will show up at their door unless they have a check ready for the remaining amount.

Banking

I love going to my mailbox at the end of our gravel driveway! It really makes my day when I receive multiple checks from clients.

Deposit your client checks the day after you receive them to keep your bank balance up and to avoid the possibility of losing them. The last thing you want to do is to have to call a client and ask them to put a payment stop on the check you lost and to please cut you a new one as soon as possible. You might as well tell them you are an idiot who loses money and to give you more — right now.

I keep a stack of deposit slips in my truck, so when checks arrive throughout the month, I make a trip to the Bank One in Brenham to deposit the funds into my corporate bank account. To keep things straight, I jot down the list of abbreviated client names and the check amounts (e.g., CCC: $1,400.25, TFE: $500.00) on the bank deposit receipt returned by the teller. Later that night during my time sheet entries into QuickBooks, I also right-click on an invoice and choose the "Receive Payments" option to enter in the deposits I made for that day. QuickBooks then automatically marks those invoices matching the client's check as "Paid." One nifty feature of QuickBooks is that it will alert you when invoices are overdue.

In my office I have a receipt case that contains all my deposit slips, invoice e-mails from online vendors, and paper receipts from local vendors. After I enter the deposit, credit, debit, or check information into QuickBooks, I then make a check mark on that paper receipt and store it in the receipt case for that calendar year. For the sake of good bookkeeping practices, and to be able to withstand any state or federal IRS audit, I have a separate receipt case for each year.

Since I use Microsoft Money to download all transactions from my company bank account, on a monthly basis I check off every debit and credit transaction from that account. This is done to verify it matches my QuickBooks register and latest stack of receipts destined for safe storage in that year's receipt case. Bank One also sends me a daily e-mail summarizing my corporate account's activities for the previous business day. I view this critical e-mail message religiously every day to make sure that all my deposits were credited and no unknown charges are being made to my business account.

Managing Cash Flow

Just like your personal bank account, money seems to go out as fast as it comes into your business account. You will want to avoid using any line of credit that may be associated with your bank account. I recommend you not set up any line of credit — that will eliminate the temptation to bleed from black to red and get into debt. Remember the big push you put on in the preparation phase of this project to eliminate as much debt as possible. Don't slide back.

Your goal should be to keep a healthy cash balance in your account to serve as a financial buffer and help you sleep at night. Keep at least a couple of thousand dollars as a minimum balance to avoid any bounced checks and to get you through tight times between client checks. Try to keep enough money in your business account to have funding available to purchase hardware and software for clients, buy learning materials to help you grow your skill sets, and, most important, to be able to pay your payroll and sales taxes on time.

Your income stream is established by the amount of billable time and materials you sold the previous month and by the schedule by which those client checks should arrive. The outgoing monetary flow is established by the expenses you have to pay and by what you choose to buy. The expenses you have to pay are, first and foremost, payroll and sales taxes. If your state or province has a sales tax on the services you provide, you will have no control over when these monthly amounts are due. Since QuickBooks can calculate the sales tax liabilities based on the amounts collected as the client checks are deposited, this should not be a problem as long as you do not spend those collected taxes on other things.

You can vary the amount of payroll taxes you must pay by varying the amount you choose to pay yourself. Since payroll taxes average around 15 percent of the *gross* amount of your paycheck, you need to make sure you keep that amount in the bank to pay to the IRS either at the end of the quarter or by the 15th of the month (depending on the size of your paychecks for that month). Since I am paying my wife and myself as full-time employees, our payroll tax liabilities are greater than $2,500 per quarter. Therefore we have to pay on a monthly basis and also file the IRS form 941 at the end of each quarter. (In Canada, payroll deductions — including CPP and federal and provincial taxes — can be anywhere from 10 to 25 percent of your gross income, depending on the income level, amount of deductible business expenses, and the province or territory in which you live. Go to the CRA website for more information at www.cra-arc.gc.ca.)

As time goes by and business grows, you will later add group health insurance to your company's benefits. This was a critical issue for me since members of my family had existing conditions that eliminated private insurance as an option. This meant we had to set up a group health-care plan through the company, and according to the laws of the state of Texas, the company needed to have at least two full-time employees. Since my wife was already putting in hours helping me with marketing, scheduling, and accounting, we made her an official full-time employee, started cutting her paychecks, and paid payroll taxes for both of us. After one quarter of her serving as the second company employee, we were able to qualify and apply for group health insurance, which covers my family despite existing conditions. The insurance companies could, however, jack up the premiums by 40 percent due to being so-called high risk.

However you are able to pull it off, you will need to provide some sort of health-care insurance for your family. Hopefully you can go the private insurance route and save on the monthly premiums. Most likely you will need to configure a group health-insurance plan through your company, but at least that amount can be directly paid by the company, whereas the private plan must be paid from your personal income after taxes.

Along with the group health-insurance premium, you must also pay for meal and travel expenses, any business-related telecommunications bills, and other online services that will come due at various times of the month. You will need to manage your cash flow wisely to cover these fixed costs, which can quickly add up to a couple of thousand dollars a month.

There will be months when business may dry up and your billable hours will be low. Fixed costs like the group health-insurance bill will still be due, so you have got to set aside funds during the busy months to cover the lean times. Consulting in both the big city and small town can be feast or famine, so think like the ant rather than the grasshopper.

Overall, try not to live by the old paycheck-to-paycheck mentality and maintain a strong consistent balance to be able pay your tax liabilities and fixed costs. You will also want to be able to shell out the cash to purchase hardware and software for client projects.

16

Clients: The Good, the Bad, and the Ugly

As a rural computer consultant, you will meet all sorts of people with various personalities and professional demeanors. For the most part, you will be pleased at the easy-going attitudes of the majority of your clients. They will be far more laid back than their city counterparts. Most will be straight talkers and not politically correct. They also will be able to see straight through any B.S. Make sure you do not talk over their heads by using too many computer-industry acronyms or highly technical jargon. This will not impress them and will most likely put them off, as it may seem you are talking down to them.

My favorite movie is *The Good, the Bad and the Ugly*, so I've decided to group the various types of clients you'll encounter into those same three categories. You will enjoy working for and will look forward to calls from clients in the "Good" category. You will learn how to tactfully dismiss those in the "Bad" group and avoid them in the future. You also will learn how to deal and work with the idiosyncrasies of clients in the "Ugly" group.

The Good

The vast majority of small-business people who will be your clients in rural towns fall into the Good group. People are just generally friendlier in small towns and are less uptight. They have fewer chips on their shoulders. They check their egos at the door and do not assume that contractors and consultants are trying to take jobs away from full-time employees.

These pleasant people are just a dream to do business with since they are genuinely glad to see you when you walk in the door to their office to resolve a computer problem. I walk into clients' offices every day and almost all of them enthusiastically say, "Hello John! How's it going?" There are very few formalities such as having to sign in and get a badge like I had to do in big-city client sites.

These Good clients are also very trusting. Since I am involved in purchasing hardware and software for them, many have given me their company credit card information, and I keep it very securely on my smartphone to be able to quickly purchase items for them when needed. Of course, I either ask them before I make large purchases or notify them immediately after I've charged smaller purchases to their cards. Many times a year, I will get a call from a client requesting that I buy them a couple of new Dell computers. As one of my services, I log on to the Dell website, configure the PCs, get them the best deal available, and put the two new computers on their company credit card. Next, I have them shipped to my home office and then forward the e-mail order message to them. When the new computers arrive, I stage them and install all the necessary antivirus and anti-spyware applications, MS Windows updates, the latest Java, and any company-specific software my client needs.

Be very careful with your clients' trust. If you store your clients' usernames, passwords, and credit card numbers on your PDA smartphone as I do, you will need to guard that data with your life. Since you will most likely be synchronizing the PDA data with MS Outlook running on your home office workstation, that security concern also applies to the Outlook PST database. If you lose your PDA smartphone with all the critical data on it, you are in deep trouble, so beware. You may want to consider using a password encryption manager application such as Password Pro.

There also may be times when a member of the Good client group has financial difficulties and has to go through a period of paying your invoices slowly. The thing to do here is have a nice sit-down with the client and have him or her set your expectations on payment times and amounts. Do not charge interest or penalties since that will sour a small-town business relationship quickly. Instead, show your support and understanding by working out a payment deal that will prove your loyalty toward this favored client. When times pick up for that client and you are again paid in full, this person will remember how you stuck with him or her during the rough times and he or she will keep you around for a long time.

Trust me on this one. My biggest and favorite client went through just this problem with a balance owing in the $5,000 range. A few months passed, and he was able to bring his company back into the black. My understanding, patience, and loyalty put me at the top of the list to get paid when the new relief funding was made available. Since that episode, that same client and I have done strong five-figure business projects and are still working well together.

The Bad

Once in a great while, you will strike a deal with a dud. Odds are good that this person got your name from a stray business card or saw your website and called you out of the blue. Of the few bad clients I have encountered working as a rural computer consultant, not one of them originated from a word-of-mouth referral from an existing Good or even Ugly client.

Over the past five years, I have only had a couple of clients that fell into the bad group. During that same time, I have also learned how to avoid taking suspect ones on as clients in the first place.

The first problem client had asked me to come take a look at his company's computer network, which was comprised of six computers, an 8-Port switch, and an ISDN router. The SOHO computing environment was a mess. The Norton AntiVirus subscription had expired months before, no MS Windows updates had been made for years, spyware was rampant, and the client's backup program had not run for months. I quickly put together a multiproject SOW and presented it to the client the next day with the data backup project as priority number one.

After putting up with him whining and complaining for more than an hour about how high the amounts were and how he could just get his son-in-law to do the work for free, he finally grudgingly agreed to have me get his backups working. This guy was obviously going to be a high-maintenance client, but since I was hungry for business back then, I proceeded with the project. After cleaning the tape drive, dumping the bad 4mm tapes, and configuring the TapeWare notification system to e-mail me the logs, I was able to get the backups working within two of the five hours quoted on the SOW. He constantly inquired about the progress of the backup job, and I told him that I got most of the problems resolved for around $200, but I'd be watching it closely.

Problems developed again due to the instability of the PC housing the tape drive, which messed up the backups a couple times, requiring me to make additional site visits to resolve the new problems. After another hour and a half billable time, the backups were stabilized. When he got the bill for $350 instead of $200, he hit the roof and complained loudly over the phone. I

explained to him that I was still in the original range of the SOW and I was doing the most important thing for him by securing his company's valuable data. This guy fussed for more than half an hour, burning my cell phone time. Finally, I told him that he would be better served by another consultant, and good luck. It was done politely and professionally, but I basically fired him.

A couple of weeks later his hard drive died, but thanks to my due diligence his son-in-law was able to reload the critical data.

I had another bad experience with a local client. This relationship started out just fine. Months into it, however, the client started paying me slowly and spread a $1,000 invoice over a six-month payout period. This bugged me a bit, but the client finally paid it off. Later the client racked up another $1,000 in upgrades and support, and then dragged it out even further. During multimonth periods with little or no payments, I found out from former employees that this client had not kept up on the health-insurance payments for the full-time employees. When these employees complained to the company (after having their insurance cards rejected during visits to their health-care providers), they were disciplined and told not to make a big deal about it.

After experiencing corporate fraud and corruption on a big scale during my contracting days at Enron, I had a hair-trigger temper and zero tolerance for that kind of crap. When I finally got the last couple of hundred from the client and later was called for additional work, I graciously but firmly told the client that due to their poor payment history and unethical business practices, I would no longer be able to provide services to them. That was another one I enjoyed firing.

Though Bad clients are few and far between, you will really appreciate being your own boss when you have the ability to just say no and dump them.

Since we try to be proactive rather than reactive in the management of our clients' computer networks, we can also be proactive in avoiding bringing on troublesome clients to start with, or clients that we don't like. Due to my negative experiences with lawyers in both my personal and professional life, I refuse to take them on as clients. The single exception to this rule of mine is with prosecuting criminal attorneys, since they fight the good fight and help keep our families safe. I do live in the real world and understand that lawyers are a necessary evil, but that doesn't mean I have to work for the devil. When they call to employ my consulting services I get a comforting feeling by informing them I refuse to support lawyers because of their negative influences in so many aspects of our daily lives. Enough said there before some attorney tries to sue me for this paragraph.

The Ugly

These clients are not in the Bad group, and can even be members of the Good group. Ugly clients can pay on time, provide great income for your company on a consistent basis, and you may really like them. The problem is, they may have some quirk or idiosyncrasy that just bugs you. One of my favorite clients pays like clockwork, has a good-flowing project list for me, and is the nicest guy to work for, but has an absolutely filthy work environment. This industrial client is stuck in the 1970s with a smoky, dirty, and smelly workplace that ruins my work clothes every time I visit the site. I am sure this is one of the last five workplaces in America where you can still smoke in the office, and he does. Sometimes, due to the material processing methods used at this client site, the smell of ammonia almost knocks me down. This client is in the Ugly group, but I wouldn't give him up for anything since he is also at the top of my Good-client group. (I hope he doesn't get upset reading this piece.)

Another client of mine just calls me once in a great while and only wants to use 15 minutes of my time, and sometimes even splurges for a whole half hour of my services. This client is an accountant and is so cheap he squeaks. Though he is a nice guy and pays within five days of receiving my bill, he is quirky, picky, and procrastinates implementing some projects for months and even years.

Nothing is perfect with any work situation and you will have to be fluid and adaptive. Personalities will sometimes clash and work environments will be uncomfortable, but you will have to be patient and flexible. Take the good with the weird, and provide a professional quality service to all of your Good and Ugly clients while trying to avoid the Bad ones.

17

Home Computer Support

With small-business clients happy with your work, you will soon be getting requests to drop by their homes and work on their home computers. This type of work can be a headache due to access issues and clients' expectations for low-cost support. However, supporting the home computers of your clients is another one of those tasks that you need to handle to keep providing the high quality customer service we talked about earlier. Your clients are, in fact, complimenting you by trusting you to go to their homes, be around their families, and help them out at the house like you did at the office. So smile, say "Sure!" and schedule the house visit as soon as it is convenient for them.

Home Computer Support Tricks of the Trade

You'll be charging the same rate for home support as you do for office support, but you may have to eat some time, since it is hard for people to understand spending three hundred dollars to get a Windows upgrade, additional memory, and new antivirus protection. I try to keep the cost down by finding them the best deal on software and hardware, along with charging them for only about 75 percent of my billable time. Think of it as additional sales time. Part of this low-cost mentality comes from the low cost of home computers, since the majority of them were bought with Windows XP Home Edition, the minimum 256MB of RAM, and no Microsoft Office, which keeps the total PC cost below $700.

Free software from your toolbox will be very useful on home computers. The two programs I constantly use are AVG Anti-Virus free version and Microsoft's Windows Defender. Also since most home users do not want to pay the $300 for MS Office to have Word and Excel, I usually install the OpenOffice suite from OpenOffice.org. They are very pleased at how the Write and Calc programs from OpenOffice look and work just like Word and Excel from Microsoft. They are really blown away when I show them how Write and Calc can read and write the equivalent Microsoft formats of .DOC and .XLS.

If your client lives out in the sticks or in a valley without high-speed broadband access, you should strongly consider taking the client's PC back to your home office to work on it there. Since most PC trouble-shooting sessions require a fast Internet connection to be able to download fixes, updates, or complete programs, a dial-up connection will not cut it. This is especially true when you are sitting in your client's living room with a dog at your feet and the children running around and the spouse asking you all sorts of questions. Trying to download 10MB of MS Windows updates over a dial-up could leave you bored to death and usually with their only phone line tied up. Odds are you will be 90 percent through with the download when your client's daughter forgets you are using the line for the Internet and picks up the phone to call her boyfriend, thereby dropping your critical connection. If I have any home computer problem that is going to take me more than 15 minutes to resolve, I let the client know that I need to work on it at my lab to get it fixed properly.

Make Sure You Back It Up

One important thing to keep in mind is that the user's data on the vast majority of home PCs is *not* backed up. This is yet another reason to take the home computer back to your office and copy its data to a large backup hard drive on your workstation. I have a big 160GB USB 2.0–connected external hard drive that I keep all my client's data backups on, which includes their home PC data. The files on their home computer can be as valuable to them as those on their office computer.

Make darn sure you back up every file and folder in My Documents, all of the music in My Music, and especially all the digital family pictures in My Pictures. I had one client's hard drive dying a slow death and I spent hours trying to salvage the thousands of digital family photos they had collected over several years. Luckily, I was able to copy all of the more than 12,533 photos before the hard drive finally gave out.

You will also want to make sure you back up their bookmarks in Internet Explorer (or whichever web browser they generally use). I had one home PC used by the wife of my client who had hundreds of bookmarks in her Favorites neatly organized in folders. She was emphatic that I not lose those. Also critical are all e-mail messages in the Inbox, Sent box, and any folder the client has created to store important messages. This also applies to the address books that contain all the e-mail addresses for family and friends. If they are running their home accounting on Quicken or MS Money, make sure you export and back up their financial data.

Keep in mind that there will probably be multiple active users on a Windows XP PC, with user accounts for each spouse and each of the kids. That means you will need the passwords to each of those accounts to repeat the backup process for each one.

Porn and Illegally Downloaded Music and Videos

Working on home PCs may be interesting when you come across funky stuff such as pornography or illegally downloaded music and videos. If you are doing a full upgrade that requires a complete backup and reload of all data, you will find yourself in a bit of a moral dilemma.

What I have done in the past is give the client a call, explain what I have found, and see what should be done with the digital contraband. I also always tell the client how the music and movie companies are coming down hard on end-user downloaders, and strongly suggest that we remove all obviously copyrighted movies and music along with any peer-to-peer file sharing applications. After I show clients articles on how some parents of kids who have illegally downloaded bootleg music and movies are getting hit with $100K lawsuits, they usually agree.

Keeping the Whole Family Happy

Along with their home PCs, many clients will also want you to support their kids' laptops.

These portables will be full of spyware, Trojan horses, and all sorts of downloaded junk that you will need to remove. My busy times working with laptops belonging to clients' college kids are Christmastime and Spring Break, when the kids bring back their nearly new computers already slowed to a crawl from the gigabytes of crap they downloaded during the semester.

Again you will want to back up all their data before you start working on laptops. Also verify the antivirus software; the majority of the college kids' laptops I work on have expired virus-definition subscriptions.

After you get your column going with the local newspaper, you will begin receiving calls for home PC support. By the time that happens, you will have it down as a new service. I have even been able to get new small-business clients from customers I originally had as home-PC customers. The combination of office and home support will probably average out to a 75 percent/25 percent split, and as a friendly rural computer consultant, you can make both service entities successful.

18

Local Allies and Time Off

If your small rural town of choice has a population of 5,000 or more, there is a strong possibility that it will have a computer repair store. In the "Pre-Move Marketing Research" section in Chapter 7, we talked about how seeking out existing computer service providers in your new area is a part of your preparation for your move. Whether it's a computer store or another consultant like yourself, they can either be your competition or your ally. Odds are, they will initially view you as a competitor, but your goal should be to make them an ally. These small-town strategic alliances can bring a host of opportunities to all involved, along with increasing the quality of computer services for the community.

My Own Local-Allies Experience

Computer Helpers is a computer store in Brenham, run by a couple of local guys in their twenties, named Harper and Jason.

They build computers for their customers with the same components used by the large computer makers and provide a three-year warranty. Harper operates the storefront full time, and Jason is the lucky one that visits all the client sites. Between the two of them, they deliver solid services and reliable computer equipment to the companies and residents of Washington County.

When I started Deans Consulting back in 2000, the guys at Computer Helpers were a bit standoffish, but were helpful when I needed to buy hardware and software. They just were not sure of me, since I was from the big city. After a couple of years went by, our business relationship warmed up and we started supporting each other in small ways. It started out with calls to each other asking about particular computer problems and solutions. I had seen and solved things they had not been exposed to, and they had hardware expertise that I lacked.

As time went on, I started getting bids from them for client workstations and comparing them to online prices from Dell. Turns out that they were able to meet or even beat Dell's low prices for the same if not better computer hardware. The deciding factor for their clients was Computer Helpers's standard three-year warranty on the computers they built. With Dell outsourcing their technical support, it had become a major nuisance to converse with the service representatives reading from the canned troubleshooting scripts. Plus, if you had to send in your computer to Dell for repair, it took many days if not weeks to get fixed and shipped back. On the very few occasions problems developed with Computer Helpers PCs, it took only one call to Harper and more often than not they were able to resolve the problem by the next day.

After five years of working with Jason and Harper, I am now purchasing complete servers from them for my larger client sites with Active Directory–based networks. Both Jason and Harper have provided me with numerous leads that developed into permanent clients. When I go on vacation, Jason covers my clients in case of emergencies during my absence. Over the years we have developed a strong working relationship that has helped grow both our businesses.

How You Can Develop Your Own Local Allies

Try your best to seed and nurture a positive relationship with the existing computer support people in your town. Put them at ease and alleviate any suspicions that you are there to take business away from them.

Instead, explain to them that what you are doing is creating a new niche of computer service. Your specialty will provide more hand-holding and personalized customer service with a fewer number of clients whereas their computer store–based business deals with a larger number of clients. Your consulting business will be more qualitative compared to their relatively quantitative business. Do not explain it to them like that, but let them know that there is plenty of work for all concerned.

The same goes for other consultants in your area. I learned that you can make an ally by having what we call a "sit-down." Have a very frank and candid conversation. Talk about how you can help each other and how a give-and-take relationship can help you both prosper, whereas an adversarial relationship can hurt both of you.

You will also want to tap into any local wireless Internet service providers, since they are common in rural areas. Here in the Brazos Valley (which includes Washington County), a company called Texas Broadband started up four years ago, and they have been a godsend to rural dial-up-bound users. Prior to that, I had been using the Washington DC–based satellite ISP called StarBand, which was expensive, unreliable, and had atrocious customer service. When I heard of Texas Broadband, I sought out the owners and immediately made an alliance with them. The deal was for a full bandwidth connection and discounted installation in exchange for a good recommendation and client referrals. After getting a 2Mb/s downstream and upstream connection with good uptime I was in Internet heaven. I even bragged to a Houston-based peer of mine, whose client had paid for a full T1 installed at his home, that I now had more usable bandwidth at my remote ranch than he did in the big city.

Over the years, Brad of Texas Broadband has referred many clients to me needing network and computer consulting. In return, I have strongly recommended them as the ISP of choice to anyone for whom DSL was not available, which was a huge number due to DSL-distance limitations. Texas Broadband went from 50 clients when we met to more than 800 as of 2005. We have worked hand in hand supporting Internet connection problems and interesting wireless throughput issues for both their clients and mine.

Another benefit of developing these informal partnerships with other local businesses related to your industry is being able to call upon them in your time of need. Many a time, I have called on Jason of Computer Helpers to pick his brain on a Windows registry issue or Brad of Texas Broadband to see if he knew what could be causing a local wireless interference problem. Both of them have also called me for advice on support issues, since this is a two-way street for technical information exchange.

Gone Fishing

Since you will be the sole provider of computer services for your consulting company, when you want to take time off and go on a vacation with your family, you cannot just put a "Gone Fishing" sign on your front door. You will need to have someone or even a group of people to help support your clients while you are gone.

I have learned to handle the vacation issue by giving my clients a two-week warning, and then during the last few days of work before my vacation, I do nothing big that could break the day after I am gone. I also make arrangements for guys like Jason and Brad to be available if my clients are in dire need of computer or networking assistance that can't wait until I'm back.

I try to be officially offline during my vacation and attempt to be completely unplugged from the IT world for both my and my family's sake. But since emergencies do happen, I tell my clients that they can leave me a voice mail or send me an e-mail message, in case the remedy to a serious problem is simple. An example of this is web and e-mail hosting issues. If any of my websites get near their disk or bandwidth quota, I am notified via e-mail, and I have a chance to fix the problem before my users stop getting e-mail or their website stops functioning. That is why, when I'm on vacation, I still carry a laptop that can connect to the Internet via my Treo 650 PDA Smartphone at 145Kbs/s. I just check e-mail once a day while on trips, but since I am a small-business person with more than 50 active clients, I have to stay on top of things. We cannot let our clients' computer environments melt down while we are away even just for a few days.

Having these alliances with other local computer professionals will help your business in many different ways and will enable you to take the time off that you and your family need from time to time.

PART 6

FINAL ISSUES

19

Critical Mass

This is the chapter I really hope you have to refer back to for guidance a few years from now because if you do, that will be a measure of your success as a rural computer consultant.

As you pick up clients and keep them happy, the numbers will grow naturally. Some of the smaller clients such as the home users may be one-timers, but most of your commercial clients will have new issues and projects that will require you to continue providing consulting services in the future.

There have been times when I don't hear from a client for months, if not a few years. Sometimes I think that clients I have not heard from in a long time got someone else to handle their computer needs, or were upset with me for some reason. Then out of the blue, I'll get a friendly call saying, "Hey John! Remember me?" and they will ask me to drop by and set up a new computer or reconfigure a network. Since many of these small companies grow slowly, they can remain static for long periods. If you have

done a good job for them, they may not need your services again for quite some time.

What I've learned to do if I have not heard from a client in more than a year is to drop by just to see how they are doing. Sometimes during those checkup visits they will say, "Glad you dropped by, and while you're here, can you …" and I'm back to work. Some clients tend to wait until problems build up before they call for help, so checkup visits to those you have not had contact with in a while can help you drum up business.

When You Are Booked Solid

As the years go by, you will accumulate dozens of clients if you serve them well. Some clients will be consistent but small sources of income and others will be occasional but large sources. The thing to remember is that you have only so many billable hours in a day. In fact, when you are serving too many clients in a day or week, your billable-hour efficiency will drop due to the travel time involved in running between client sites. That is why this business model of doing many little jobs for several clients would not work in an urban or metropolitan area. Remember that in Houston I was barely able to visit three clients in an eight-hour period due to the horrendous traffic on both the freeways and regular streets. In rural Washington County, it is not unusual for me to hit ten client sites in one day.

But eventually (whether it is in two or ten years), your client base will consume all your available time. Once you reach this point, I recommend that you be very clear with any new person or company who calls you about your services. Do not put them off for weeks (like some doctors do) by telling them your first opening is sometime next month. Instead, take this opportunity to be very picky and explain to these prospects that you are booked solid and are not taking on new clients at this time. Opportunities to take on interesting new clients may come up if things lighten up a bit, but if those new calls come from companies that sound like they may fit into the Bad or even the Ugly client group we talked about earlier, it will be easy for you to just say no.

Time to Train Others

When you do hit that saturation point, it may be time to keep your ears open for new consultants in the area who want to do what you do. There may also be an employee at one of your client sites who has expressed interest in learning to be a rural computer consultant.

One of my favorite original clients back in 2000 had a brilliant guy working as a chemist who really wanted to get into the IT industry. Over the years I had him tag along with me while I upgraded PCs, set up servers, and resolved networking issues. Later, he started up his consulting business on the side, and I helped him along the way. In fact, during his first year, I was able to refer new home-PC business to him, which helped lighten my load. When I went on vacations, I was able to have him handle all my home users, which gave me good peace of mind while I was "offline."

If you picked the right town, it will grow over the years, and you will need to either defer business to other new consultants or even take on a new employee. This would be a change from my business model, but it can work. During my Paranet days I had enough of interviewing people and dealing with the problems that employees generate, so I have stuck with only two employees in my own business — me doing the consulting work and my wife doing everything else. This keeps things simple and calm.

Taking on new professional talent and billing them out under your good name will have both risks and rewards. Doing all the work yourself like I do keeps everything in your control and all the knowledge in your head. When new people are brought in as full-time employees, you will have a specific amount and dates for payroll to be made, which is probably different from the payroll-as-you-make-it flexible schedule you will have been following the first few years. You will also have to deal with the need for group health insurance with a larger monthly premium.

Other increased responsibilities are payroll tax issues and workers' compensation reporting. Taking on a full-time billable consultant can help generate more income but will also bring up new responsibilities and liabilities for your small company. Your cash flow will also become more complicated. Since our business can be feast or famine, working a single-person company is advantageous as it allows you to sometimes take little or no payroll during the lean times. With a full-time employee, all the payroll flexibility goes away, as the employee will expect a steady paycheck.

If you bring on contract talent and pay them on a percentage basis via the IRS 1099 schedules, you'll eliminate the payroll and other responsibilities, but contractors can be hard to find and good ones are often already booked when you need them. There were times when I was able to utilize consulting talent from professionals I previously worked with who were between jobs, and it usually worked out well. However, contract workers cannot be consistently relied upon to help grow your company.

The critical mass problem will eventually come your way and you will have to deal with it using one of the methods discussed above. I truly hope you have to deal with this sooner rather than later as a successful rural computer consultant.

Epilogue

We must be the masters of our own destinies. We have the precious freedom to make decisions and choose our paths in life. As a rural computer consultant, I've found that the free-enterprise system works in rural areas as well as, if not better than, in big cities. You'll likely find the same. Rural-town-based small businesses are simpler to deal with and more enjoyable to work at day in and day out. Life becomes less hectic and stressful since complex contracts strewn with lawyer-ese are replaced with an honest handshake. Instead of wasting so many hours a week sitting in city traffic staring at red brake lights, you can enjoy your country drives on open scenic roads through pastures or forests.

One of the reasons I wrote this book was that I could not find any other book on the Amazon or Barnes & Noble websites that described how to start and run a computer consulting business in rural areas. After five successful years of being a rural computer consultant (and spending the last year training others on how to do this), I felt I had to get it all on paper and see how it sounded. As I started with a basic outline and began to construct the flow of this book, the main thing that kept popping up was the need to emphasize how one has to be the jack-of-all-trades in the computer field.

Since this is the only way to be a successful small-town computer consultant, you will have to do many little jobs for several clients a week. The more of the 40 skill sets you possess, the more services you can offer and the more billable hours you will be able to rack up. What you will not find is just one or two small-town clients who will contract 20 to 40 hours a week of your services at consulting rates. Your day will consist of numerous small troubleshooting sessions and fast projects that will take 30 minutes at one client and a couple of hours at the next.

Review and analyze the list of 40 skill sets and identify the ones that best fit your capabilities, along with those that match the needs of the clientele in your area. Troubleshooting computer problems will always be your first foot in a new client's door, so make sure you have trained in, studied, and gained real experience fixing computer troubles. Resolving Microsoft Windows–related problems is a must and should be first on your list of services to offer.

My life experiences have taught me that the harder you work, the luckier you get. Over the years, I have had friends and even family tell me they thought I was one of the luckiest people they have known, and how things just seem to pop up for me. While I agree that timing is crucial and opportunities must be appreciated, being able to foresee upcoming or developing opportunities and prepare oneself to engage those timely opportunities is not luck but rather effort, planning, and dedication.

Your preparation for this big change of life is absolutely critical. To change both your homestead and your career within the same year can be very stressful. Remember the family issues we discussed and make darn sure you have your spouse's full support for the whole project. This includes the move to the country, the time you will be spending starting a new business, and the risk of fiscal tightness for many months, if not years. Diligently research and carefully pick your small town to find just the right fit for your family and the new business you are planning to start. A critical part of this planning is the financial preparation for both home and business expenditures, so work those Excel spreadsheets as realistically as possible to avoid going back into the red. The business plan is another task that cannot be overlooked and should be thought out in

detail to help you address any and all small-business issues.

When you get to the country and start up your business as a rural computer consultant, you will be faced with what seem like a hundred things to get accomplished each day. First, settle your family and help them get comfortable with their new environment, and then jump into the business start-up venture. Take seriously the recommendations to join local organizations such as the chamber of commerce, and keep your ears open for opportunities to join the Rotary Club. Spend the money to get your accounting with QuickBooks set up properly so you can start out on the right foot in the bookkeeping department. This includes setting up your tax status and payment schedules even though you may be earning very little at first.

Be careful not to burn through your start-up capital too fast. Purchase just the critical items you will need, such as the website, laptop, and crucial software to snag your first clients. Since the majority of your on-duty time at your new business will be consumed performing nonbillable administrative tasks, use it wisely by correctly setting up the corporation or LLC, along with all other office-related projects. Time to get these overhead jobs completed will dwindle fast when new clients start calling.

Once the ball gets rolling, you will understand what I was talking about when it comes to self-employment discipline. Stay on top of things using your smartphone by putting projects in your tasks list and appointments in your calendar. Don't arrive late for appointments, and try to avoid rescheduling them if possible. Do your time sheet in QuickBooks and document all expenses every evening without fail. Remember those free services, such as backup verification, that will help your new clients and bring in even more clients. Be able to quickly respond when clients ask for project estimates with a comprehensive scope of work that lays out the prioritized list of projects along with their approximate costs.

Since being a rural computer consultant is a service business, you will have to deal directly with all sorts of personalities on a daily basis. Be flexible and smile when you deal with the difficult clients because they also have small-town contacts. Remember, we live and die by the all-powerful word of mouth. Our reputation is our livelihood.

Though supporting home computers may be troublesome due to limited access and clients' general reluctance to spend the money, it is still required of us. Try to see other local computer professionals as peers and support, rather than as competition. They can be of great help to you when difficult computer problems arise or when you need someone to cover for your next vacation.

Finally, do what you love to do. All successful people are great at what they do and work so hard at it because they get up every morning and can't wait to get after it. If you really enjoy the computer industry, like dealing with people on a one-to-one basis, and would like to do all this in a small-town environment, then becoming a rural computer consultant may be for you. Use this book as a guide and a reference to help you implement this life-changing adventure.

Though I believe God has a plan for each and every one of us, we can still make our own destinies here on earth with hard work and good planning.

Good luck.

The following Checklists, Worksheets, Samples, and Resource Lists are included on the enclosed CD-ROM for use on a Windows-based PC. The forms are in MS Word or Excel as well as in PDF formats.

Checklists

- Small-Town Assessment
- Home Office/Mobile Office Checklist
- Marketing Campaign Materials
- Skill Set Checklist

Worksheets

- Start-up Costs
- Marketing Contact List
- Scope of Work

Samples

- Skill Set Checklist — Sample
- CD-ROM Business Card (Flash presentation)

Resource Lists

- John Deans's Newspaper Column (with links)
- Programs in the Network Toolbox